200 Light vegetarian dishes

hamlyn | **all colour cookbook**

200 Light
vegetarian dishes

An Hachette UK Company
www.hachette.co.uk

First published in Great Britain in 2015 by Hamlyn
a division of Octopus Publishing Group Ltd
Endeavour House, 189 Shaftesbury Avenue
London WC2H 8JY
www.octopusbooks.co.uk

ISBN: 978-0-600-62895-8

A CIP catalogue record for this book is available from the
British Library.

Printed and bound in China.

1 2 3 4 5 6 7 8 9 10

Both metric and imperial measurements have been given
in all recipes. Use one set of measurements only, and not a
mixture of both.

Standard level spoon measurements are used in all recipes
1 tablespoon = 15 ml spoon
1 teaspoon = 5 ml spoon

Ovens should be preheated to the specified temperature
– if using a fan-assisted oven, follow the manufacturer's
instructions for adjusting the time and temperature.

Fresh herbs, medium eggs and freshly ground black
pepper should be used unless otherwise stated.

This book includes dishes made with nuts and nut
derivatives. It is advisable for people with known allergic
reactions to nuts and nut derivatives or those who may be
potentially vulnerable to these allergies, such as pregnant
and nursing mothers, invalids, the elderly, babies and
children, to avoid dishes made with these. It is prudent
to check the labels of all pre-prepared ingredients for the
possible inclusion of nut derivatives.

contents

introduction   6

recipes under 200 calories   18

recipes under 300 calories   70

recipes under 400 calories   142

recipes under 500 calories   200

index   236

acknowledgements   240

introduction

introduction

this series

The Hamlyn All Colour Light Series is a collection of handy-sized books, each packed with over 200 healthy recipes in a variety of cuisines and topics to suit your needs.

The books are designed to help those people who are trying to lose weight by offering a range of delicious recipes that are low in calories but still high in flavour. The recipes show a calorie count per portion, so you will know exactly what you are eating. These are recipes for real and delicious food, not ultra-slimming meals, so they will help you maintain your new healthier eating plan for life. They must be used as part of a balanced diet, with the cakes and sweet dishes eaten only as an occasional treat.

how to use this book

All the recipes in this book are clearly marked with the number of calories (kcal) per serving. The chapters cover different calorie bands: under 500 calories, under 400 calories, and so on. There are variations on each recipe at the bottom of the page – note the calorie count as they do vary and can sometimes be more than the original recipe.

The figures assume that you are using low-fat versions of dairy products, so be sure to use skimmed milk and low-fat yogurt. They have also been calculated using lean meat, so make sure you trim meat of all visible fat and remove the skin from chicken breasts. Use moderate amounts of oil and butter for cooking and low-fat/low-calorie alternatives whenever you can.

Don't forget to take note of the number of portions each recipe makes and divide up the quantity of food accordingly, so that you know exactly how many calories you are consuming.

Be careful about accompaniments and side dishes that will also add to calorie content.

Above all, enjoy trying out the new flavours and exciting recipes that this book has to offer. Rather than dwelling on the thought that you are denying yourself your usual unhealthy treats, think of your new regime as a positive step towards a new you. Not only will you lose weight and feel more confident as a result, but your health will benefit, the

condition of your hair and nails will improve and you will take on a healthy glow.

the risks of obesity

Up to half of women and two-thirds of men are overweight or obese in the developed world today. Being overweight not only can make us unhappy with our appearance, but can also lead to serious health problems, including heart disease, high blood pressure and diabetes.

When someone is obese, it means they are overweight to the point that it could start to seriously threaten their health. In fact, obesity ranks as a close second to smoking as a possible cause of cancer. Obese women are more likely to have complications during and after pregnancy, and people who are overweight or obese are also more likely to suffer from coronary heart disease, gallstones, osteoarthritis, high blood pressure and type 2 diabetes.

how can I tell if I am overweight?

The best way to tell if you are overweight is to work out your body mass index (BMI). If using metric measurements, divide your weight in kilograms (kg) by your height in metres (m), then divide the result by your height again. (For example, if you weigh 70 kg and are 1.7 m tall, the calculation would be 70 ÷ 1.7 = 41.2 ÷ 1.7 = 24.2.) If using imperial measurements, divide your weight in pounds (lb) by your height in inches (in), then divide the result by your height again and multiply by 703. Then compare the figure to the list below (these figures apply to healthy adults only).

Less than 20	underweight
20–25	healthy
26–30	overweight
Over 31	obese

As we all know by now, one of the major causes of obesity is eating too many calories.

what is a calorie?

One of the major causes of obesity is eating too many calories. Our bodies need energy to stay alive, grow, keep warm and be active. We get the energy we need to survive from the food and drinks we consume – more specifically, from the fat, carbohydrate, protein and alcohol that they contain.

A calorie (cal), as anyone who has ever been on a diet will know, is the unit used to

measure how much energy different foods contain. A calorie can be scientifically defined as the energy required to raise the temperature of 1 gram of water from 14.5°C to 15.5°C. A kilocalorie (kcal) is 1,000 calories and it is, in fact, kilocalories that we usually mean when we talk about the calories in different foods.

Different food types contain different numbers of calories. For example, a gram of carbohydrate (starch or sugar) provides 3.75 kcal, protein provides 4 kcal per gram, fat provides 9 kcal per gram and alcohol provides 7 kcal per gram. So, fat is the most concentrated source of energy – weight for weight, it provides just over twice as many calories as either protein or carbohydrate – with alcohol not far behind. The energy content of a food or drink depends on how many grams of carbohydrate, fat, protein and alcohol are present.

how many calories do we need?

The number of calories we need to consume varies from person to person, but your body weight is a clear indication of whether you are eating the right amount. Body weight is simply determined by the number of calories you are eating compared to the number of calories your body is using to maintain itself and needed for physical activity. If you regularly consume more calories than you use up, you will start to gain weight, as extra energy is stored in the body as fat.

Based on our relatively inactive modern-day lifestyles, most nutritionists recommend that

women should aim to consume around 2,000 calories (kcal) per day and men an amount of around 2,500. Of course, the amount of energy required depends on your level of activity: the more active you are, the more energy you need to maintain a stable weight.

a healthier lifestyle

To maintain a healthy body weight, we need to expend as much energy as we eat. To lose weight, energy expenditure must therefore exceed intake of calories, so exercise is a vital tool in the fight to lose weight. Physical activity doesn't just help control body weight; it also helps to reduce appetite and is known to have beneficial effects on the heart and blood, which will help to protect against cardiovascular disease.

Many adults claim not to enjoy doing exercise or say that they simply don't have

Some activities will use up more energy than others. The following list shows some examples of the energy a person weighing 60 kg (132 lb) would expend doing the following activities for 30 minutes:

activity	energy
Ironing	69 kcal
Cleaning	75 kcal
Walking	99 kcal
Golf	129 kcal
Fast walking	150 kcal
Cycling	180 kcal
Aerobics	195 kcal
Swimming	195 kcal
Running	300 kcal
Sprinting	405 kcal

the time to fit it into their hectic schedules. The easiest way in which to increase physical activity is by incorporating it into your daily routines, perhaps by walking or cycling instead of driving (particularly for short journeys), taking up more active hobbies such as gardening, rambling or swimming, and taking small and simple steps such as choosing the stairs instead of the lift whenever possible.

As a general guide, adults should aim to undertake at least 30 minutes of moderate-intensity exercise, such as a brisk walk, five times a week. The 30 minutes do not have to be taken all at once: three sessions of 10 minutes are equally beneficial. Children and young people should be encouraged to take at least 60 minutes of moderate-intensity exercise every day.

make changes for life

The best way to lose weight is to try to adopt healthier eating habits that can be easily maintained as a way of life, not just when you are trying to slim down. Aim to lose no more than 1 kg (2 lb) per week to ensure you lose only your fat stores. People who go on crash diets lose lean muscle as well as fat and are much more likely to put the weight back on again soon afterwards.

For women, the aim is to reduce daily calorie intake to around 1,500 kcal to achieve the desired weight loss, then to stick to around 2,000 per day thereafter to maintain this weight. Regular exercise will also make a huge difference: the more you can burn, the less you will need to diet.

improve your diet

For most of us, simply adopting a more balanced diet will reduce our calorie intake and lead to weight loss. Follow these simple recommendations:

• Eat more starchy foods such as bread, potatoes, rice and pasta. Assuming these replace the fattier foods you usually eat and you don't smother them with oil or butter, this will reduce the amount of fat and increase the amount of fibre in your diet. Try to use wholegrain rice, pasta and flour, as the energy from these foods is released more slowly in the body, making you feel fuller for longer.

• Eat more fruit and vegetables, aiming for at least five portions of different fruits and vegetables a day (excluding potatoes).

• As long as you don't add extra fat to fruit and vegetables in the form of cream, butter or oil, these changes will help reduce your fat intake and increase the amount of fibre and vitamins you consume.

who said vegetables must be dull?

Eat fewer sugary foods, such as biscuits, cakes and chocolate bars. This will also help reduce your fat intake. If you want something sweet, have some fresh or dried fruit instead.

Reducing the amount of fat in your diet means you will consume fewer calories overall. Choosing low-fat versions of dairy products such as skimmed milk and low-fat yogurt doesn't necessarily mean your food will be tasteless. Low-fat versions are available for most dairy products, including milk, cheese, crème fraîche, yogurt and even cream and butter.

simple steps to reduce your fat intake

Few of us have an iron will, so when you are trying to cut down make it easier on yourself by following these steps:

• Serve small portions to start with. You may feel satisfied when you have finished, but if you are still hungry you can always go back for more.

• Once you have served up your meal, put away any leftover food before you sit down to eat. Avoid putting heaped serving dishes

13

on the table as you will undoubtedly pick, even if you feel satisfied with what you have already eaten.

- Eat slowly and really savour your food; you are more likely to feel full when you have finished. If you rush a meal, you may still feel hungry afterwards.

- Make an effort with your meals – the food doesn't have to be low on taste as well as in calories. You will feel more satisfied with a meal you thoroughly enjoyed and will be less likely to look for comfort in a bag of crisps or a bar of chocolate.

- Plan your meals in advance to make sure you have all the ingredients you need. Rummaging around in the cupboards when you are hungry is unlikely to result in a healthy, balanced meal.

- Keep healthy and interesting snacks to hand for those moments when you need something to pep you up. You don't need to succumb to a chocolate bar if there are other tempting treats on offer.

what is a vegetarian diet?

The Vegetarian Society defines a vegetarian as 'Someone who lives on a diet of grains, pulses, nuts, seeds, vegetables and fruits, with or without the use of dairy products and eggs. A vegetarian does not eat any meat, poultry, game, fish, shellfish or by-products of slaughter.' People may choose to follow a vegetarian diet for various reasons, including religious, health, ethical and environmental.

Today, being a vegetarian, cooking for a vegetarian in your family or choosing to have a couple of meat-free days a week is so easy – with supermarkets and health food shops offering a range of ingredients for making tasty and satisfying vegetarian dishes. Many people perceive vegetarian cooking as being time-consuming and featuring heavy stews of beans and lentils, nut loaves and omelettes. This book aims to dispel that myth. It provides 200 recipes to help you create simple, flavourful vegetarian feasts, with inspirational ideas for easy, nutritious dishes for breakfast and brunch, starters and snacks, main meals, soups and stews, salads and sides, breads and baking, and desserts. There's sure to be something here to please all tastes, vegetarian and non-vegetarian alike.

ingredients

For vegetarians, avoiding certain products can be tricky. For example, animal fat and ingredients such as gelatine may be used in manufactured foods. Rennet, which is extracted from the stomach lining of cows, is often used in cheese making. Also, some jars of curry paste may contain shrimp. In many cases, there are vegetarian alternatives to these ingredients, so it is advisable to take time to check the food labels.

cheese

Cheese is a good source of protein for vegetarians, but always check the label to ensure that it is suitable for vegetarians and doesn't contain animal rennet. Some hard cheeses are still made with animal rennet, although increasingly cheese is being made with 'microbial enzymes', widely used in the industry because they are a consistent and inexpensive coagulant.

The term 'microbial enzyme' means that it is a synthetically developed coagulant, while the term 'vegetable rennet' indicates one derived from a vegetable source. Soft cheeses such as cream cheese and cottage cheese are manufactured without rennet. Some cottage cheeses, however, may contain gelatine, which is derived from animal sources.

The following are cheeses suitable for vegetarians and useful to keep in the fridge:

goats' cheese Made from goats' milk, this cheese has a tangy flavour and can be either soft and creamy or hard, so can be suitable for grating.

feta This crumbly white Greek cheese is traditionally made from ewes' milk or a mixture of ewes' and goats' milk, but is now sometimes made using cows' milk. Salty in flavour and is perfect in salads and with couscous or pasta.

mozzarella A fresh or unripened Italian cheese traditionally made from water buffaloes' milk. A firm but creamy cheese, it tastes like fresh milk with a sour edge. It melts well and has a unique stretchiness, making it the classic pizza-topping cheese.

cheddar Made from cows' milk, a lot of Cheddar is now produced using vegetarian rennet. Mature Cheddar has great flavour.

vegetarian pasta cheese This is a great vegetarian alternative to Parmesan cheese for use in risottos or pasta dishes.

taleggio From Northern Italy, this mildly flavoured whole cows' milk cheese has a soft texture and a fruity, creamy character.

ricotta This soft Italian curd cheese is made from whey, which is drained and then lightly 'cooked'. It is creamy with a slightly grainy texture and delicate flavour. Relatively low in fat, it is used in many Italian dishes.

ensuring a balanced diet

A vegetarian diet can supply all the nutrients needed for health and vitality, and eating vegetarian can make it easier to achieve the desired '5 a day' consumption of fresh fruit and vegetables.

Although a vegetarian diet doesn't guarantee better health, any risk associated with eating red meat is obviously eliminated. Unless you are vegan, you will most likely be consuming other animal products, including eggs, cheese, butter, cream and milk, but it is important to avoid the common trap of over-compensating for the lack of meat by consuming, in particular, large amounts of cheese, which is high in saturated fats that can lead to heart disease.

To get the most from our food, buy good-quality ingredients and avoid processed foods. Always purchase fruit, vegetables and herbs in the freshest condition possible to gain the maximum nutritional benefits. There is a far greater choice now when it comes to buying organic, but it remains the more expensive option. It is always worthwhile purchasing organic free-range eggs, but beyond that you can choose which organic produce to buy according to your budget and what looks good on the day.

It can be useful to eat food from the following five food 'groups'.

• protein

Pulses (peas, beans and lentils) are excellent and inexpensive sources of protein and also contain essential minerals such as iron, zinc and calcium.

Soya products, which include tofu and Quorn™, contain a form of 'mycoprotein' and these are available as mince, burgers, fillets and sausages.

Eggs, dairy products, nuts and seeds contain zinc, valuable calcium and iron, as well as protein.

• fruit and vegetables

Aim to eat at least five portions of fruit and vegetables a day, where one portion weighs about 80 g (3 oz).

Choose a wide variety of different coloured fruit and vegetables to provide a balanced mix of nutrients.

day, where one portion is a 200 ml (7 fl oz) glass of milk, a 150 ml (¼ pint) pot of yogurt or a 30 g (1 oz) piece of cheese. Alternatives include rice milk, dried figs, nuts, green vegetables and soya products, such as tofu.

• vitamins and minerals

Iron is vital for the maintenance of healthy red blood cells and to prevent anaemia. Vegetarian sources include eggs, leafy green vegetables, wholemeal bread, molasses, dried fruit (especially apricots), pulses, fortified breakfast cereals, peanut butter and pumpkin, sesame and sunflower seeds. Iron from vegetable sources is not as easily absorbed as that from animal sources. If eaten with food rich in vitamin C, the body's absorption of iron is enhanced. Drink fruit juice with your breakfast cereal or squeeze fresh lemon juice on green vegetables and salads.

Remember that the only sure-fire way of knowing what you are eating is to make your own meals, so start cooking now and enjoy some fabulous and healthy vegetarian food.

• carbohydrate-rich foods

Potatoes, pasta, rice and pulses provide sustained energy from carbohydrates, as well as B vitamins and fibre. One-third of your food intake should be made up of carbohydrate, so try to eat one food from this group each meal.

• dairy products or alternatives

These are needed for protein and calcium. At least three portions should be eaten each

recipes under 200 calories

fruity summer smoothie

Calories per serving **103**
Makes **4 x 300 ml (½ pint)
    glasses**
Preparation time **2 minutes**

2 **peaches**, halved, pitted and
    chopped
300 g (10 oz) **strawberries**
300 g (10 oz) **raspberries**
400 ml (14 fl oz) **skimmed**
    or **semi-skimmed milk**
ice cubes

Put the peaches in a blender or food processor with
the strawberries and raspberries and blend to a smooth
purée, scraping the mixture down from the sides of
the bowl if necessary.

Add the milk and blend the ingredients again until the
mixture is smooth and frothy. Pour the milkshake over
the ice cubes in tall glasses.

For soya milk & mango shake, replace the peaches,
strawberries and raspberries with the flesh of 2 large
ripe mangoes and the juice of 2 oranges. Purée as
above, then pour in 400 ml (14 fl oz) soya milk, blend
and serve over ice cubes as above. **Calories per
serving 138**

rocket, pear & pecorino salad

Calories per serving **195**
Serves **4**
Preparation time **10 minutes**

250 g (8 oz) **rocket leaves**
2 **pears**
75 g (3 oz) **pecorino cheese shavings**

Dressing
1 teaspoon **Dijon mustard**
2 tablespoons **cider vinegar**
2 tablespoons **olive oil**
salt and **pepper**

Make the dressing by whisking the mustard, cider vinegar and oil. Season to taste with salt and pepper.

Put the rocket in a large salad bowl. Finely slice the pears and add them to the rocket. Add the dressing to the salad and toss carefully to mix.

Layer most of the pecorino shavings through the rocket and pear salad, garnish with the remaining shavings and serve.

For rocket, apple & balsamic salad, combine 250 g (8 oz) rocket, 1 finely sliced green apple and 75 g (3 oz) pecorino cheese shavings in a large salad bowl. Whisk together 2 tablespoons aged balsamic vinegar and 3 tablespoons olive oil. Add the dressing to the salad, toss carefully to mix and serve immediately. Calories per serving 204

braised black cabbage & borlotti

Calories per serving **187**
Serves **4**
Preparation time **10 minutes**
Cooking time **30 minutes**

1.5 kg (3 lb) **cavolo nero
   (black cabbage)**
3 tablespoons **olive oil**
2 **garlic cloves**, thinly sliced
¼ teaspoon **crushed dried
   chillies**
400 g (13 oz) can **borlotti
   beans**, rinsed and drained
salt

Remove the thick stalks of the cabbage by holding the stems with one hand and using the other hand to strip away the leaves. Discard the stalks. Cook the leaves in a saucepan of boiling water for 15 minutes until just tender, then drain thoroughly.

Heat the oil in a large frying pan over a low heat. Add the garlic, crushed chillies and borlotti beans and cook for 5 minutes, then stir in the cooked cabbage. Season with salt and cook, stirring, for 6–8 minutes until the cabbage has completely wilted and absorbed the flavours. Serve immediately.

For spinach with pine nuts, follow the recipe above from the second step onwards, replacing the borlotti beans with 50 g (2 oz) pine nuts. Use 500 g (1 lb) baby spinach instead of the cabbage, toss into the pan raw and cook, stirring, for 2–3 minutes until wilted. Stir a light grating of nutmeg into the cooked spinach before serving. **Calories per serving 204**

veggie stir-fry with pak choi

Calories per serving **186**
(**not including rice**)
Serves **4**
Preparation time **10 minutes**
Cooking time **5–7 minutes**

8 small **pak choi**, about
625 g (1 ¼ lb) in total
1 tablespoon **groundnut oil**
2 **garlic cloves**, thinly sliced
2.5 cm (1 inch) piece of fresh
root ginger, peeled and
finely chopped
200 g (7 oz) **sugar snap
peas**, sliced diagonally
200 g (7 oz) **asparagus tips**,
sliced in half lengthways
200 g (7 oz) **baby corn**, sliced
in half lengthways
125 g (4 oz) **podded
edamame beans** or
200 g (7 oz) **bean sprouts**
150 ml (¼ pint) **sweet teriyaki
sauce**

Cut the pak choi in half, or into thick slices if large, and put in a steamer basket. Lower into a shallow saucepan of boiling water so that the pak choi is not quite touching the water. Cover and steam for 2–3 minutes or until tender. Alternatively, use a bamboo or electric steamer.

Heat a large wok or frying pan over a high heat until smoking hot, add the oil, garlic and ginger and stir-fry for 30 seconds. Add the vegetables and stir continuously for 2–3 minutes or until beginning to wilt.

Pour over the sweet teriyaki sauce, toss to combine and serve immediately with the steamed pak choi and some steamed rice, if liked.

For sweet chilli vegetable stir-fry, heat the oil in the wok and stir-fry 1 thinly sliced onion with the garlic and ginger. Add 1 carrot, cut into thin matchsticks, and 200 g (7 oz) sliced mushrooms and stir-fry for 2 minutes. Stir in 200 g (7 oz) bean sprouts and 300 g (10 oz) shredded spinach for a further minute until wilted. Stir in 200 ml (7 fl oz) sweet chilli stir-fry sauce and serve immediately with the pak choi or cooked noodles. **Calories per serving 235**

squash, kale & mixed bean soup

Calories per serving **182**
  (not including garlic bread)
Serves **6**
Preparation time **15 minutes**
Cooking time **45 minutes**

1 tablespoon **olive oil**
1 **onion**, finely chopped
2 **garlic cloves**, finely chopped
1 teaspoon **smoked paprika**
500 g (1 lb) **butternut
  squash**, halved, deseeded,
  peeled and diced
2 **small carrots**, peeled
  and diced
500 g (1 lb) **tomatoes**,
  skinned (optional) and
  roughly chopped
400 g (13 oz) can **mixed
  beans**, rinsed and drained
900 ml (1½ pints) hot
  vegetable stock
150 ml (¼ pint) **half-fat
  crème fraîche**
100 g (3½ oz) **kale**, torn
  into bite-sized pieces
salt and **pepper**

Heat the oil in a saucepan over a medium-low heat,
add the onion and fry gently for 5 minutes. Stir in the
garlic and smoked paprika and cook briefly, then add
the squash, carrots, tomatoes and mixed beans.

Pour in the stock, season with salt and pepper and
bring to the boil, stirring frequently. Reduce the heat,
cover and simmer for 25 minutes or until the vegetables
are cooked and tender.

Stir in the crème fraîche, then add the kale, pressing it
just beneath the surface of the stock. Cover and cook
for 5 minutes or until the kale has just wilted. Ladle into
bowls and serve with warm garlic bread, if liked.

For cheesy squash, pepper & mixed bean soup,
make as above, replacing the carrots with 1 cored,
deseeded and diced red pepper. Pour in the stock, then
add 65 g (2½ oz) Parmesan cheese rinds and season.
Cover and simmer for 25 minutes. Stir in the crème
fraîche but omit the kale. Discard the Parmesan rinds,
ladle the soup into bowls and top with grated Parmesan.
Calories per serving 241

cauliflower & chickpea curry

Calories per serving **180**
 **(not including rice
 and raita)**
Serves **4**
Preparation time **10 minutes**
Cooking time **20 minutes**

1 tablespoon **groundnut oil**
8 **spring onions**, cut into 5 cm
 (2 inch) lengths
2 teaspoons **grated garlic**
2 teaspoons **ground ginger**
2 tablespoons **medium
 curry powder**
300 g (10 oz) **cauliflower
 florets**
1 **red pepper**, cored,
 deseeded and diced
1 **yellow pepper**, cored,
 deseeded and diced
400 g (13 oz) can **chopped
 tomatoes**
400 g (13 oz) can **chickpeas**,
 rinsed and drained
salt and **pepper**

Heat the oil in a large nonstick frying pan over a
medium heat. Add the spring onions and stir-fry for
2–3 minutes. Add the garlic, ginger and curry powder
and stir-fry for 20–30 seconds until fragrant. Now add
the cauliflower and peppers and stir-fry for a further
2–3 minutes.

Stir in the tomatoes and bring to the boil. Cover, reduce
the heat to medium and simmer for 10 minutes, stirring
occasionally. Add the chickpeas, season to taste and
bring back to the boil. Remove from the heat and serve
immediately with steamed rice and mint raita, if liked.

For broccoli & black-eye bean curry, follow the
recipe above replacing the cauliflower with 300 g
(10 oz) broccoli florets and the chickpeas with a 400 g
(13 oz) can black-eye beans. **Calories per serving 179**

thai veg salad

Calories per serving **180**
Serves **4**
Preparation time **10 minutes,
    plus cooling**
Cooking time **2 minutes**

250 g (8 oz) **cherry tomatoes,**
    quartered
1 **Lebanese cucumber,**
    thinly sliced
1 **green papaya** or **green
    mango**
1 large **red chilli,** deseeded
    and thinly sliced
150 g (5 oz) **bean sprouts**
4 **spring onions,** trimmed
    and thinly sliced
small handful of **Thai basil
    leaves**
small handful of **mint leaves**
small handful of fresh
    coriander leaves
4 tablespoons **unsalted
    peanuts,** roughly chopped

Chilli dressing
2 tablespoons **sweet chilli
    sauce**
2 tablespoons **light soy sauce**
2 tablespoons **lime juice**
2 tablespoons **lime
    marmalade,** warmed

Make the dressing. Put all the ingredients in a small
saucepan and warm over a low heat, stirring, until
combined. Leave to cool.

Put the tomatoes, cucumber, papaya or mango, chilli,
bean sprouts, spring onions and herbs in a bowl. Add
the dressing and toss well. Transfer to a platter. Sprinkle
over the peanuts and serve immediately.

For Thai salad wraps, serve the salad with large
iceberg lettuce leaves. Spoon a little salad onto the
leaves, roll up and dip into the chilli dressing. To cool
the chilli heat, omit the sweet chilli sauce in the
dressing. **Calories per serving 171**

cannellini with sage & tomato

Calories per serving **179**

Serves **4**

Preparation time **10–15 minutes, plus soaking** (optional)

Cooking time **15 minutes** for canned beans; **45 minutes** for fresh; 1¾ **hours** for dried

250 g (8 oz) shelled **fresh cannellini beans**, or 200 g (7 oz) **dried cannellini beans**, soaked in cold water overnight, drained and rinsed, or 2 x 400 g (13 oz) cans **cannellini beans**, rinsed and drained

1 **bay leaf** (optional)

2 **garlic cloves**, unpeeled, or 1 **garlic clove**, chopped

2 teaspoons **olive oil**

1 **red onion**, thinly sliced

5 **sage leaves**, roughly chopped

pinch of crushed **dried chillies**

2 **tomatoes**, skinned and chopped

salt

extra-virgin olive oil, for drizzling (optional)

Put the fresh beans, if using, into a saucepan, pour in enough cold water to cover by about 5 cm (2 inches) and add the bay leaf, if using, and unpeeled garlic cloves. Bring to the boil and skim off any scum that rises to the surface. Reduce the heat to a simmer and cook, uncovered, for 25–30 minutes, or until tender. Drain, reserving the garlic cloves. If using presoaked dried beans, cook as for the fresh beans, but they will take about 1½ hours to become tender. The canned beans are ready to use.

Heat the oil in a large, heavy-based frying pan over a low heat. Add the red onion, sage and crushed chillies and cook, stirring occasionally, for 10 minutes until the onion is softened. If you cooked the beans from scratch, squeeze the garlic flesh out of the skins into the pan. If using canned beans, simply add the chopped garlic to the pan. Cook, stirring, for 1 minute, then add the beans and the tomatoes. Season with salt and cook, stirring, for 3–5 minutes. Serve drizzled with a little extra-virgin olive oil, if liked.

courgette, feta & mint salad

Calories per serving **169**
Serves **4**
Preparation time **10 minutes**
Cooking time **10 minutes**

3 **green courgettes**
2 **yellow courgettes**
olive oil
small bunch of **mint**
40 g (1 ½ oz) **feta cheese**
salt and **pepper**

Dressing
2 tablespoons **olive oil**
grated rind and juice of
  1 **lemon**

Slice the courgettes thinly lengthways into long
ribbons. Drizzle with oil and season with salt and pepper.
Heat a griddle pan to very hot and grill the courgettes in
batches until marked by the griddle on both sides, then
transfer to a large salad bowl.

Make the dressing by whisking together the oil and
the grated lemon rind and juice. Season to taste with
salt and pepper.

Roughly chop the mint, reserving some leaves for the
garnish. Carefully mix together the courgettes, mint
and dressing. Transfer them to a large salad bowl,
then crumble the feta over the top, garnish with the
remaining mint leaves and serve.

For marinated courgette salad, thinly slice
3 courgettes lengthways and put them in a non-
metallic bowl with ½ deseeded and sliced red chilli,
4 tablespoons lemon juice, 1 crushed garlic clove and
4 tablespoons olive oil. Season to taste with salt and
pepper. Leave the salad to marinate, covered, for at
least 1 hour. Roughly chop a small bunch of mint, toss
with the salad and serve immediately. **Calories per
serving 151**

vegetables with sweet chilli sauce

Calories per serving **168**
Serves **4**
Preparation time **10 minutes**
Cooking time **5 minutes**

250 g (8 oz) **chestnut mushrooms**, trimmed and halved
2 tablespoons **cornflour**
2 tablespoons **groundnut oil**
1 tablespoon chopped fresh **root ginger**
2 **garlic cloves**, thinly sliced
½ teaspoon **salt**
2 **red peppers**, cored, deseeded and cut into chunks
4 small **pak choi**, cut in half lengthways
2 tablespoons **Chinese rice wine** or **dry sherry**
1 tablespoon **dark soy sauce**
1 tablespoon **sweet chilli sauce**
4 **spring onions**, thinly sliced

Place the mushrooms in a bowl with the cornflour and toss to coat. Set aside.

Heat the oil in a wok over a high heat until the oil starts to shimmer. Add the ginger, garlic and salt and stir quickly, then add the mushrooms, red peppers and pak choi and stir-fry for 2–3 minutes until just tender.

Stir in the rice wine, soy and sweet chilli sauces and spring onions and cook for 1 more minute, until the sauce has thickened.

red cabbage slaw

Calories per serving **159**
  (not including bread)
Serves **4**
Preparation time **20 minutes,**
  plus marinating

500 g (1 lb) **red cabbage**
1 **red onion**
1 **raw beetroot**
2 **carrots**
1 **fennel bulb**
2 tablespoons chopped
  parsley or **dill**
75 g (3 oz) **raisins** or **sultanas**

Dressing
6 tablespoons **natural yogurt**
1 tablespoon **cider vinegar** or
  white wine vinegar
2 teaspoons **sweet German**
  mustard or **Dijon mustard**
1 teaspoon **clear honey**
1 **garlic clove**, crushed
salt and **pepper**

Trim the stalk end of the red cabbage and finely shred the cabbage. Cut the red onion in half and slice it thinly. Peel the beetroot and carrots and cut them both into thin matchsticks or grate coarsely. Halve the fennel bulb and shred it finely.

Put all the prepared vegetables, chopped parsley or dill and raisins or sultanas in a large salad bowl and toss them with your hands to combine well.

Make the dressing. Mix the yogurt with the vinegar, mustard, honey, crushed garlic, a pinch of salt and plenty of pepper. Pour this dressing over the slaw, mix well and leave to marinate for at least 1 hour. Serve the slaw with rye or sourdough bread.

For crunchy chilli slaw, finely slice 250 g (8 oz) white cabbage and 250 g (8 oz) red cabbage. Cut 1 carrot into thin ribbons with a peeler and thinly slice 1 red onion and 1 fennel bulb. Make a dressing by mixing together 3 tablespoons sweet chilli sauce, 1 tablespoon soy sauce, 1 tablespoon barbecue sauce, 2 tablespoons olive oil and the juice of 2 limes. Toss the salad in the dressing and allow to stand for at least 30 minutes for the flavours to infuse before serving. **Calories per serving 151**

white bean soup provençal

Calories per serving **126**
  (not including bread)
Serves **6**
Preparation time **15 minutes,**
  plus soaking
Cooking time **20 minutes**

3 tablespoons **olive oil**
2 **garlic cloves**, crushed
1 small **red pepper**, cored,
  deseeded and chopped
1 **onion**, finely chopped
250 g (8 oz) **tomatoes**,
  finely chopped
1 teaspoon finely chopped
  thyme
400 g (13 oz) can **haricot** or
  cannellini beans, drained
  and rinsed
600 ml (1 pint) **vegetable**
  stock
2 tablespoons finely chopped
  flat-leaf parsley
salt and **pepper**

Heat the oil in a large heavy-based saucepan, add the garlic, red pepper and onion and cook over a medium heat for 5 minutes or until softened.

Add the tomatoes and thyme and cook for 1 minute. Add the beans and pour in 600 ml (1 pint) water and the stock. Bring to the boil, then reduce the heat, cover and simmer for 15 minutes until the tomatoes are softened.

Sprinkle in the parsley and season with salt and pepper. Serve immediately in warmed soup bowls with fresh, crusty bread.

For Spanish white bean soup, add 100 g (3½ oz) diced chorizo sausage when frying the onions, garlic and red pepper. Stir in 1 teaspoon pimentón (Spanish smoked paprika) or 1 teaspoon mild chilli powder. Cook for 1 minute until fragrant, then add the tomatoes and continue with the recipe as above.
Calories per serving 203

trivandrum beetroot curry

Calories per serving **115**
Serves **4**
Preparation time **15 minutes**
Cooking time **25–30 minutes**

1 tablespoon **groundnut oil**
1 teaspoon **black mustard seeds**
1 **onion**, chopped
2 **garlic cloves**, chopped
2 **fresh red chillies**, deseeded and finely chopped
8 **curry leaves**
1 teaspoon **ground turmeric**
1 teaspoon **cumin seeds**
1 **cinnamon stick**
400 g (13 oz) **raw beetroots**, peeled and cut into matchsticks
200 g (7 oz) can **chopped tomatoes**
100 ml (3½ fl oz) **reduced-fat coconut milk**
juice of 1 **lime**
salt
chopped **coriander leaves**, to garnish

Heat the oil in a wok or saucepan over a medium heat. Add the mustard seeds and as soon as they begin to 'pop' (after a few seconds), add the onion, garlic and chillies. Cook for about 5 minutes until the onion is soft and translucent.

Add the remaining spices and the beetroots. Fry for a further 1–2 minutes, then add the tomatoes, 250 ml (8 fl oz) water and a pinch of salt. Simmer everything for 15–20 minutes, stirring occasionally, until the beetroot is tender.

Stir in the coconut milk and simmer for a further 1–2 minutes until the sauce has thickened. Stir in the lime juice and check the seasoning. Garnish with chopped coriander and serve immediately.

For spiced beetroot salad, thickly slice 625 g (1¼ lb) cooked beetroot and arrange on a wide serving platter with 1 very thinly sliced red onion and a large handful of rocket leaves. Make a dressing by whisking 200 ml (7 fl oz) reduced-fat coconut milk with 1 tablespoon curry powder and 4 tablespoons each of very finely chopped coriander and mint. Season to taste and drizzle over the beetroot salad. Toss to mix well and serve. **Calories per serving 132**

malaysian spicy cauliflower

Calories per serving **118**
Serves **4**
Preparation time **10 minutes**
Cooking time **10 minutes**

2 tablespoons **groundnut oil**
1 **red chilli**, deseeded and
  finely chopped
1 **onion**, thickly sliced
2 **garlic cloves**, chopped
1 teaspoon **salt**
500g (1 lb) **cauliflower**, cut
  into florets then sliced

Heat the oil in a wok over a high heat until the oil starts to shimmer. Add the chilli, onion and garlic and stir-fry for 1 minute.

Add the salt and cauliflower. Stir well to combine all the flavours then sprinkle with 3 tablespoons water, cover and steam for 3–4 minutes, until tender.

For spicy cauliflower soup, start the recipe as above, adding 250 g (8 oz) peeled and diced floury potatoes with the cauliflower. Once all the flavours are tossed together, pour in 1 litre (1 ¾ pints) vegetable stock. Simmer for 15 minutes, then blend until smooth. Serve with a drizzle of chilli oil. **Calories per serving 186**

garden salad

Calories per serving **134**
Serves **4**
Preparation time **10 minutes**

½ **cucumber**
250 g (8 oz) **cherry tomatoes**
250 g (8 oz) **baby leaf mix**,
   such as **mizuna, baby**
   chard, lollo rosso, purslane
   and **oak-leaf lettuce**
1 **avocado**
50 g (2 oz) **pitted black olives**

Dressing
1 teaspoon **Dijon mustard**
2 tablespoons **cider vinegar**
3 tablespoons **olive oil**
salt and **pepper**

Peel and slice the cucumber and halve the tomatoes. Mix the salad leaves with the cucumber and tomatoes in a large salad bowl. Stone and peel the avocado, cut the flesh into dice and add to the bowl with the olives.

Make the dressing by whisking together the mustard, vinegar and oil. Season to taste with salt and pepper.

Pour the dressing over the salad, toss carefully to combine and serve.

chilli kale

Calories per serving **95**
Serves **4**
Preparation time **8 minutes**
Cooking time **17 minutes**

1 tablespoon **olive oil**
1 **garlic clove**, crushed
1 large **white onion**, chopped
500 g (1 lb) **curly kale**, stalks
   removed and leaves chopped
2 teaspoons **lime juice**
1 **red chilli**, deseeded and
   chopped
salt and **black pepper**

Heat the oil in a wok over a moderate heat. Add the garlic and onion and sauté for about 10 minutes or until the onion is translucent.

Add the curly kale and stir-fry for another 5 minutes.

Stir in the lime juice and chilli, season with salt and pepper to taste and serve immediately.

For chilli cabbage, replace the curly kale with 500 g (1 lb) cabbage. Discard the stalks and tough outer leaves, then chop the leaves before frying with the garlic and onion and finishing as above. This dish also works well with spring greens. **Calories per serving 87**

strawberry & cucumber salad

Calories per serving **122**
Serves **4**
Preparation time **10 minutes**,
   plus chilling

1 large **cucumber**, halved
   lengthways, deseeded and
   thinly sliced
250 g (8 oz) **strawberries**,
   halved or quartered if large

Balsamic dressing
1 tablespoon **balsamic
   vinegar**
1 teaspoon **wholegrain
   mustard**
1 teaspoon **clear honey**
3 tablespoons **olive oil**
salt and **pepper**

Put the cucumber slices and strawberry halves or
quarters in a shallow bowl.

Put all the dressing ingredients in a screw-top jar,
season to taste with salt and pepper, and shake well.

Pour the salad dressing over the cucumber and
strawberries. Toss gently, then cover and chill for
5–10 minutes before serving.

For cucumber & dill salad, prepare the cucumber
as specified above, then put the slices in a colander
set over a plate or in the sink. Sprinkle with 2 teaspoons
salt and leave to stand for 20–30 minutes, to allow the
excess moisture to drain away. Rinse under cold running
water, then drain thoroughly and transfer to a shallow
serving dish. In a bowl, mix together 4 tablespoons
thick Greek yogurt, 1 teaspoon white wine vinegar
and 2 tablespoons chopped dill. Season well with
pepper. Pour over the cucumber, toss gently to
combine and serve garnished with dill sprigs.
Calories per serving 51

peperonata

Calories per serving **143**
Serves **4**
Preparation time **10 minutes,
plus preparing the peppers**
Cooking time **45 minutes**

2 large **red peppers**,
grilled, skinned, cored
and deseeded
2 large **yellow peppers**,
grilled, skinned, cored
and deseeded
2 teaspoons **olive oil**
1 small **onion**, finely chopped
2 **garlic cloves**, finely chopped
400 g (13 oz) can **plum
tomatoes**, roughly chopped
6 large **basil leaves**, torn
extra-virgin olive oil, for
drizzling (optional)
salt

Cut the peppers into wide strips and set aside.

Heat the oil in a heavy-based saucepan over a low
heat. Add the onion and cook, stirring occasionally,
for 10 minutes. Add the garlic and cook, stirring, for
1 minute. Add the tomatoes and their juice and the
pepper strips. Season with salt and bring to the boil.
Reduce the heat to a gentle simmer and cook, stirring
occasionally, for 25 minutes.

Stir the basil into the pan and cook for 5–10 minutes
until the sauce has reduced. Drizzle with extra-virgin
olive oil before serving, if liked. Serve immediately as
a side dish. Alternatively, serve cold as an antipasto.

For caper & lemon peperonata, follow the recipe
as above, also adding 2 tablespoons capers and
the grated zest of 1 lemon to the pan with the basil.
Calories per serving 144

marinated tofu & mushroom salad

Calories per serving **185**
Serves **4**
Preparation time **15 minutes**,
  plus marinating
Cooking time **5 minutes**

250 g (8 oz) **firm tofu**
500 g (1 lb) **mushrooms**,
  including **enoki, shiitake,**
  wood ear and **oyster**

Marinade
1 **garlic clove**, finely chopped
2 cm (¾ inch) fresh **root**
  ginger, peeled and finely
  sliced
5 tablespoons **soy sauce**
1 tablespoon **mirin**
2 tablespoons **sweet chilli**
  sauce
1½ tablespoons **sesame oil**
2 **star anise**

To garnish
5 **spring onions**, finely sliced
2 tablespoons **sesame seeds**,
  toasted

Make the marinade. Mix the garlic and ginger with
the soy sauce, mirin, sweet chilli sauce and oil. Add
the star anise.

Put the tofu in a non-metallic dish, pour over the
marinade, cover and refrigerate for at least 2 hours
or overnight if possible.

Cut the mushrooms into bite-sized pieces and sauté
in a hot saucepan for 1 minute. Cut the marinated tofu
into 2 cm (¾ inch) squares, mix with the mushrooms
and pour over the remaining marinade. Garnish with
finely sliced spring onions and sesame seeds and
serve immediately.

For tofu & rice salad, cook 200 g (7 oz) sushi rice
according to the instructions on the packet. While
the rice is still warm season it with 100–150 ml
(3½–5 fl oz) rice seasoning vinegar. Cut 500 g (1 lb)
mixed mushrooms into bite-sized pieces and cook briefly,
then mix through the rice with 1 carrot cut into julienne
strips and a small bunch of finely sliced spring onions.
Mix the salad well, garnish with 100 g (3½ oz) finely
sliced deep-fried bean curd and toasted sesame seeds
and serve immediately. **Calories per serving 350**

spring vegetable salad

Calories per serving **131**
Serves **4**
Preparation time **10 minutes**
Cooking time **10 minutes**

200 g (7 oz) **fresh** or
   frozen peas
200 g (7 oz) **asparagus**,
   trimmed
200 g (7 oz) **sugar snap peas**
2 **courgettes**
1 **fennel bulb**

Dressing
grated rind and juice of
   1 **lemon**
1 teaspoon **Dijon mustard**
1 teaspoon **clear honey**
1 tablespoon chopped
   flat-leaf parsley
1 tablespoon **olive oil**

Put the peas, asparagus and sugar snap peas in a saucepan of salted boiling water and simmer for about 3 minutes. Drain, then refresh under cold running water.

Cut the courgettes into long, thin ribbons and thinly slice the fennel. Transfer all the vegetables to a large salad bowl and mix together.

Make the dressing by whisking together the lemon rind and juice, mustard, honey, flat-leaf parsley and oil in another bowl. Toss the dressing through the vegetables and serve.

For beetroot dressing to serve with the spring vegetable salad, prepare the vegetables as above and set aside. Finely slice ½ red onion and 1 garlic clove. Heat 2 tablespoons olive oil in a saucepan over a medium heat and gently cook the onion and garlic. Add 4 precooked beetroot and 6 roughly chopped sun-blushed tomatoes and cook for a further 3 minutes. When the onions start to colour deglaze the pan with 2 tablespoons balsamic vinegar. Cook for 1 minute, then add 100 ml (3½ fl oz) vegetable stock. Reduce the stock by a quarter, then leave to cool. Transfer the stock to a blender or food processor and whiz until smooth. Season with salt and pepper and add up to 2 tablespoons cream until the dressing reaches a drizzling consistency. Drizzle the dressing over the vegetables and serve. **Calories per serving 258**

rocket & parmesan salad

Calories per serving **139**
Serves **4–6, as a side dish**
Preparation time **5 minutes**

250 g (8 oz) **rocket leaves**
20 g (¾ oz) finely grated
  Parmesan cheese
40 g (1½ oz) **Parmesan**
  cheese shavings

Dressing
4 tablespoons **lemon juice**
2 tablespoons **olive oil**
½ teaspoon **Dijon mustard**
salt and **pepper**

Make the dressing by whisking the lemon juice, oil and mustard together. Season to taste with salt and pepper.

Put the rocket in a large salad bowl, sprinkle over the grated Parmesan and mix lightly. Pour over the dressing and toss to combine. Garnish the salad with the Parmesan shavings and serve.

For rocket salad with chive dressing, blanch a bunch of chives in boiling water for 30 seconds until bright green. Refresh immediately in cold water. Squeeze out all the excess water, roughly chop and transfer to a blender jug. Add 50 ml (2 fl oz) mayonnaise, 1 tablespoon white wine vinegar and salt and pepper to taste. Blend until smooth, adjusting the consistency with 1 tablespoon warm water if necessary. Mix 250 g (8 oz) rocket with a thinly sliced fennel bulb, pour over the dressing, toss together and serve immediately. **Calories per serving 114**

okra, pea & tomato curry

Calories per serving **176**
Serves **4**
Preparation time **5 minutes**
Cooking time **about 20 minutes**

1 tablespoon **groundnut oil**
6–8 **curry leaves**
2 teaspoons **black mustard seeds**
1 **onion**, finely diced
2 teaspoons **ground cumin**
1 teaspoon **ground coriander**
2 teaspoons **curry powder**
1 teaspoon **ground turmeric**
3 **garlic cloves**, finely chopped
500 g (1 lb) **okra**, cut on the diagonal into 2.5 cm (1 inch) pieces
200 g (7 oz) **fresh** or **frozen peas**
2 ripe **plum tomatoes**, finely chopped
salt and **pepper**
3 tablespoons grated **fresh coconut**, to serve

Heat the oil in a large nonstick wok or frying pan over a medium heat. Add the curry leaves, mustard seeds and onion. Stir-fry for 3–4 minutes until fragrant and the onion is starting to soften, then add the cumin, ground coriander, curry powder and turmeric. Stir-fry for a further 1–2 minutes until fragrant.

Add the garlic and okra, and increase the heat to high. Cook, stirring, for 2–3 minutes, then add the peas and tomatoes. Season to taste, cover and reduce the heat to low. Cook gently for 10–12 minutes, stirring occasionally, until the okra is just tender. Remove from the heat and sprinkle over the grated coconut just before serving.

For spiced seeded pea & tomato pilaf, place 300 g (10 oz) basmati rice in a medium saucepan with 2 teaspoons dry-roasted cumin seeds, 1 tablespoon crushed dry-roasted coriander seeds, 2 teaspoons black mustard seeds, 200 g (7 oz) fresh or frozen peas and 3 peeled, deseeded and finely chopped tomatoes. Add 650 ml (1 pint 2 fl oz) hot vegetable stock, bring to the boil and season to taste. Reduce the heat to low, cover the pan and cook gently for 10–12 minutes or until all the liquid has been absorbed. Remove from the heat and allow to stand, covered and undisturbed, for 10–15 minutes. Fluff up the grains with a fork and serve. **Calories per serving 341**

pak choi with chilli & ginger

Calories per serving **48**
Serves **4**
Preparation time **5 minutes**
Cooking time **5 minutes**

1 tablespoon **groundnut oil**
½ fresh **red chilli**, sliced
   into rings
1 tablespoon chopped fresh
   root ginger
large pinch of **salt**
500 g (1 lb) **pak choi**, leaves
   separated
¼ teaspoon **sesame oil**

Heat the oil in a wok over a high heat until the oil starts to shimmer. Add the chilli, ginger and salt and stir-fry for 15 seconds.

Tip the pak choi into the wok and stir-fry for 1 minute, then add 100 ml (3½ fl oz) water and continue stirring until the pak choi is tender and the water has evaporated. Toss in the sesame oil and serve immediately.

shaved fennel & radish salad

Calories per serving **87**
Serves **4**
Preparation time **10 minutes**

2 **fennel bulbs**, about 650 g
   (1 lb 5 oz) in total
300 g (10 oz) **radishes**
2 tablespoons roughly
   chopped **parsley**

Dressing
4 tablespoons **lemon juice**
2 tablespoons **olive oil**
salt and **pepper**

Slice the fennel and radishes as thinly as possible
on a mandolin or with a knife, reserving the fennel
fronds for the garnish. Toss together in a large salad
bowl with the parsley.

Make the dressing by whisking together the lemon
juice and oil. Season to taste with salt and pepper.

Add the dressing to the salad and toss gently to
mix. Garnish with the reserved feathery fennel fronds
and serve.

For pickled fennel salad, mix together 3 tablespoons
cider vinegar, 1 tablespoon toasted cumin seeds and
400 ml (14 fl oz) water in a small saucepan. Bring
to the boil and season to taste with salt and pepper.
Immediately pour the liquid over 650 g (1 lb 5 oz) thinly
sliced fennel and leave to cool. Drain the pickled fennel
and serve as a side salad or as an accompaniment to
grilled fish. **Calories per serving 40**

curried cabbage & carrot stir-fry

Calories per serving **84**
  (not including rice)
Serves **4**
Preparation time **10 minutes**
Cooking time **about**
  15 minutes

1 tablespoon **groundnut oil**
4 **shallots,** finely chopped
2 teaspoons peeled and finely
  grated fresh **root ginger**
2 teaspoons finely grated
  garlic
2 fresh **long green chillies,**
  halved lengthways
2 teaspoons **cumin seeds**
1 teaspoon **ground turmeric**
1 teaspoon **coriander seeds,**
  crushed
1 large **carrot,** coarsely grated
300 g (10 oz) **green** or **white**
  cabbage, finely shredded
1 tablespoon **curry powder**
salt and **pepper**

Heat the oil in a large nonstick wok or frying pan
over a low heat. Add the shallots, ginger, garlic and
chillies and stir-fry for 2–3 minutes until the shallots
have softened. Add the cumin seeds, turmeric and
crushed coriander seeds and stir-fry for 1 minute.

Increase the heat to high and add the carrot and
cabbage, tossing well to coat in the spice mixture.
Add the curry powder and season to taste. Cover the
pan and cook over a medium-low heat for 10 minutes,
stirring occasionally. Remove from the heat and serve
immediately with steamed rice.

For speedy coconut, carrot & cabbage curry, heat
1 tablespoon groundnut oil in a large wok and add
2 tablespoons medium curry paste, 2 chopped garlic
cloves and 1 sliced onion and stir-fry for 3–4 minutes
until softened. Chop 2 large carrots into 1 cm (½ inch)
pieces and add to the onion mixture with 300 g (10 oz)
roughly chopped cabbage, 300 ml (½ pint) vegetable
stock and 200 ml (7 fl oz) reduced-fat coconut milk.
Bring to the boil, reduce the heat to medium and cook
for 12–15 minutes or until the carrot is tender. Remove
from the heat and serve garnished with chopped
coriander. **Calories per serving 145**

recipes under 300 calories

baked figs with goats' cheese

Calories per serving **201**
Serves **4**
Preparation time **10 minutes**
Cooking time **10–12 minutes**

8 firm but ripe **fresh figs**
75 g (3 oz) **soft goats' cheese**
8 **mint leaves**
2 tablespoons **extra-virgin olive oil**
salt and **pepper**

Rocket salad
150 g (5 oz) **baby rocket leaves**
1 tablespoon **extra-virgin olive oil**
1 teaspoon **lemon juice**
salt and **pepper**

Cut a cross in the top of each fig without cutting through the base. Put 1 teaspoonful of the goats' cheese and a mint leaf in each fig. Transfer to a roasting tin, then season with salt and pepper and drizzle with the oil.

Bake in a preheated oven, 190°C (375°F), Gas Mark 5, for 10–12 minutes until the figs are soft and the cheese has melted.

Make the rocket salad. Put the baby rocket leaves in a bowl. Whisk together the oil, lemon juice, salt and pepper and drizzle over the leaves. Serve with the figs.

For figs stuffed with mozzarella & basil, replace the goats' cheese with 125 g (4 oz) sliced mozzarella and use basil leaves instead of the mint leaves. Continue the recipe as above. Serve with sprigs of watercress instead of the rocket salad. **Calories per serving 253**

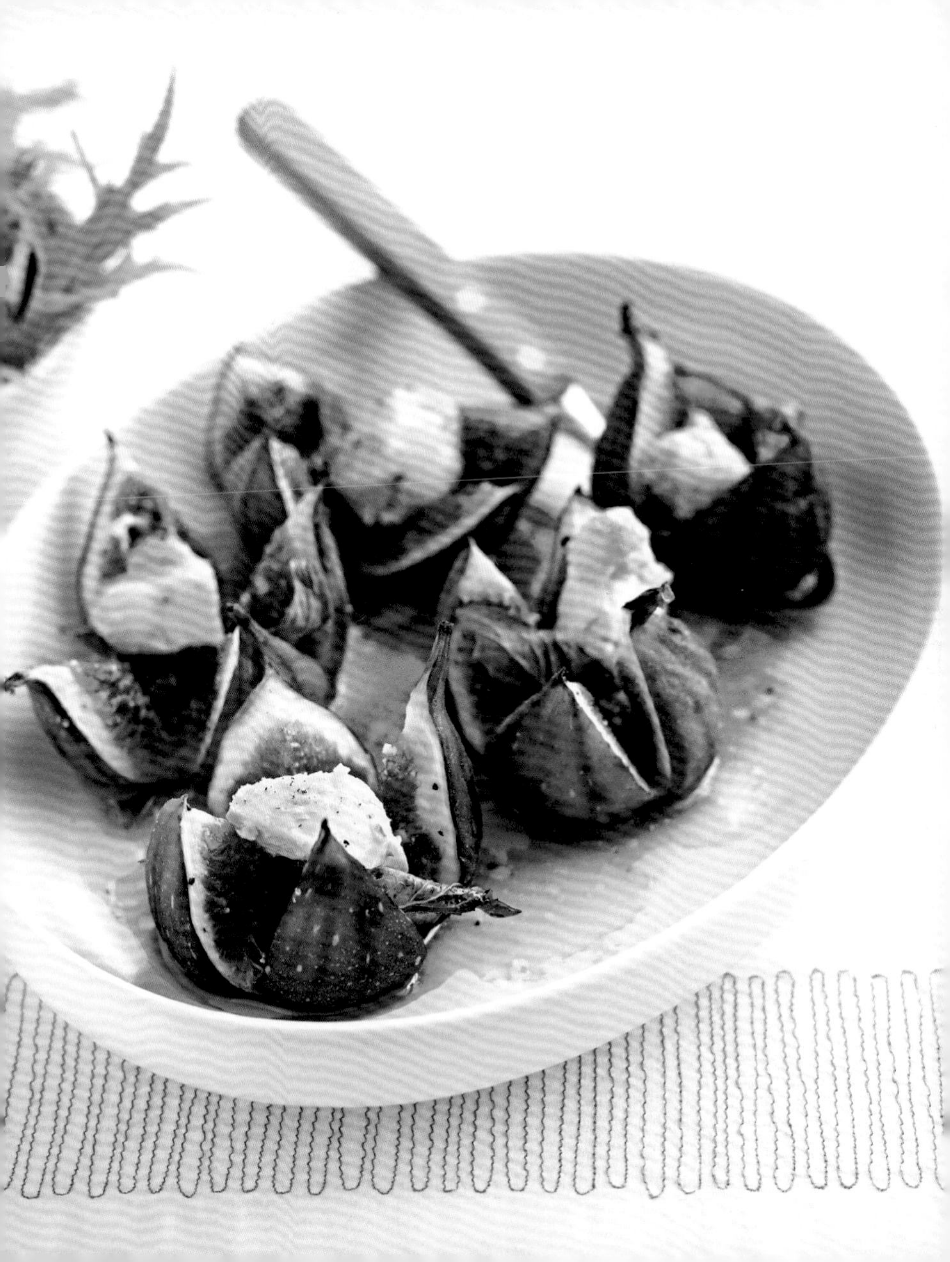

spinach & pea frittata

Calories per serving **201**
   (not including salad)
Serves **4**
Preparation time **10 minutes**
Cooking time **25 minutes**

1 tablespoon **olive oil**
1 **onion**, thinly sliced
150 g (5 oz) **baby spinach
   leaves**
125 g (4 oz) shelled **fresh
   or frozen peas**
6 **eggs**
salt and **pepper**

Heat the oil in a heavy-based, ovenproof, nonstick
23 cm (9 inch) frying pan over a low heat. Add the
onion and cook for 6–8 minutes until softened, then
stir in the spinach and peas and cook for a further
2 minutes, or until any moisture released by the spinach
has evaporated.

Beat the eggs in a bowl and season lightly with salt
and pepper. Stir in the cooked vegetables, then pour the
mixture into the pan and quickly arrange the vegetables
so that they are evenly dispersed. Cook over a low heat
for about 8–10 minutes, or until all but the top of the
frittata is set.

Transfer the pan to a preheated very hot grill and cook
about 10 cm (4 inches) from the heat source until the
top is set but not coloured. Give the pan a shake to
loosen the frittata, then transfer to a plate to cool. Serve
slightly warm or at room temperature, accompanied by
a green salad, if liked.

For courgette, pea & cheese frittata, follow the
first step as above, but replace the spinach with
1 large courgette, coarsely grated. Add 4 tablespoons
freshly grated Parmesan cheese and 100 g (3½ oz)
cubed mozzarella cheese to the raw egg mixture with
the vegetables and cook as above. **Calories per
serving 312**

pickled vegetable salad

Calories per serving **209**
Serves **4**
Preparation time **20 minutes,
   plus cooling**
Cooking time **20 minutes**

8 small **shallots**
1 small **cauliflower**
1 **red pepper**
150 ml (¼ pint) **white wine
   vinegar**
150 g (5 oz) **green beans**
150 g (5 oz) **sugar snap peas**
75 g (3 oz) **watercress**
4 tablespoons **olive oil**
salt and **pepper**

Trim the shallots and cut the cauliflower into small
florets. Core and deseed the pepper and cut the flesh
into 2 cm (¾ inch) squares.

Put 1 litre (1¾ pints) cold water and the vinegar into
a heavy-based saucepan, bring to the boil and add the
cauliflower, pepper and shallots. Return the liquid to the
boil and boil for 2 minutes. Take the saucepan off the
heat and leave the vegetables to cool in the liquid.

Trim the beans and sugar snap peas and blanch
in lightly salted boiling water. Refresh them in cold
water and drain.

When the pickling liquid is cool, strain the vegetables
and mix them with the beans, peas and watercress in
a large salad bowl. Dress with the olive oil, season to
taste with salt and pepper and serve.

For pickled cucumber & chilli salad, cut 2 cucumbers
in half lengthways and remove the seeds by running
a small teaspoon along the centre. Slice the cucumber
diagonally and place in a non-metallic bowl. Add
1 tablespoon finely sliced pickled ginger, 1 deseeded
and finely sliced red chilli and 5 finely sliced spring
onions. Put 100 g (3½ oz) caster sugar, 75 ml (3 fl oz)
rice wine vinegar and 400 ml (14 fl oz) cold water in a
heavy-based saucepan and bring to the boil. Allow to
cool, then pour the liquid over the cucumbers and leave
to stand for at least 1 hour. The pickled cucumbers will
keep for up to one week in a covered container in the
refrigerator. **Calories per serving 123**

tomato & mozzarella salad

Calories per serving **212**
Serves **4**
Preparation time **15 minutes**

500 g (1 lb) **ripe tomatoes**,
  preferably different types,
  such as **heirloom** and
  cherry and **plum**
about 3 tablespoons **olive oil**
2 tablespoons **aged balsamic**
  vinegar
small handful of **basil leaves**
150 g (5 oz) **mini mozzarella**
  balls
salt and **pepper**

Cut half the tomatoes into thick slices and the other half into wedges. Arrange the slices on a large serving plate, slightly overlapping each other.

Put the tomato wedges in a bowl and drizzle with most of the olive oil and balsamic vinegar. Season to taste with salt and pepper. Mix carefully and arrange on top of the tomato slices.

Add the basil leaves and mozzarella balls to the tomato wedges. Drizzle the salad with more olive oil and balsamic vinegar, season to taste with salt and pepper and serve.

For tomato & pasta salad, cook 250 g (8 oz) fusilli or penne until just tender. Refresh in cold water. Chop 500 g (1 lb) tomatoes into chunks and stir through the still warm pasta, coat with olive oil and season to taste with salt and pepper. Mix through a large handful of torn basil leaves, garnish with Parmesan cheese shavings and serve. **Calories per serving 366**

smoked tofu & apricot sausages

Calories per serving **232**
  **(not including chips
  and relish)**
Serves **4**
Preparation time **20 minutes**
Cooking time **10 minutes**

225 g (7½ oz) **smoked tofu**
2 tablespoons **olive oil** or
  vegetable oil, plus a little
  extra for frying
1 large **onion**, roughly
  chopped
2 **celery sticks**, roughly
  chopped
100 g (3½ oz) **no-soak dried
  apricots**, roughly chopped
50 g (2 oz) **breadcrumbs**
1 **egg**
1 tablespoon chopped **sage**
salt and **pepper**
flour, for dusting

Pat the tofu dry on kitchen paper and cut into chunks.
Heat the oil in a frying pan and fry the onion and
celery for 5 minutes until softened. Tip them into a
food processor and add the tofu and apricots. Blend
the ingredients to a chunky paste, scraping down the
mixture from the sides of the bowl if necessary.

Tip the mixture into a mixing bowl and add the
breadcrumbs, egg and sage. Season with salt and pepper
and beat well until everything is evenly combined.

Divide the mixture into eight portions. Using lightly
floured hands, shape each portion into a sausage shape,
pressing the mixture together firmly.

Heat a little oil in a nonstick frying pan and fry the
sausages for about 5 minutes, until they are golden.
Serve with chunky chips and a spicy relish, if liked.

For a spicy apple relish to serve with the sausages,
peel and core 4 cooking apples and cut them into
chunks. Place in a saucepan with 100 ml (3½ fl oz)
dry cider, 1 cinnamon stick, 2 teaspoons light soft
brown sugar and ½ teaspoon crushed chillies. Cover
and cook over a low heat until the apples have broken
up into a pulp. Allow to cool before serving. **Calories
per serving 78**

beetroot, spinach & orange salad

Calories per serving **221**
Serves **4**
Preparation time **20 minutes,
    plus cooling**
Cooking time **1–2 hours**

500 g (1 lb) uncooked
    beetroots, preferably of
    a similar size
2 **garlic cloves**, peeled
    and left whole
handful of **oregano leaves**
1 teaspoon **vegetable oil**
1 tablespoon **balsamic
    vinegar**
200 g (7 oz) **baby spinach
    leaves**
2 **oranges**, peeled, white
    pith removed and cut into
    segments
salt and **pepper**

Vinaigrette
1 tablespoon **balsamic
    vinegar**
1 teaspoon **Dijon mustard**
4 tablespoons **olive oil**
pinch of **sugar** (optional)

Put the whole beetroots in the centre of a large piece of foil, along with the garlic and oregano. Sprinkle with pepper and drizzle over the vegetable oil and vinegar. Gather up the foil loosely and fold over at the top to seal it. Place on a baking sheet and bake in a preheated oven, 200°C (400°F), Gas Mark 6, for 1–2 hours (depending on how large the beetroots are) until tender. Unwrap the foil parcel and leave the beetroots to cool before peeling and slicing them. Discard the garlic.

Make the vinaigrette. Mix together the balsamic vinegar and mustard in a small bowl. Season with a little salt and pepper. Gradually add the olive oil, whisking constantly, until smooth and well combined. Taste and adjust the seasoning as needed, adding a pinch of sugar to reduce the acidity, if liked, bearing in mind the sweetness of the roasted beetroots. Whisk again until the sugar has dissolved. Alternatively, put all the vinaigrette ingredients in a screw-top jar, seal tightly and shake vigorously until well combined.

Put the spinach in a large bowl, and gently toss together with the beetroots and oranges. Drizzle over the vinaigrette and sprinkle with pepper.

For beetroot, spinach & goats' cheese salad,

prepare and roast the beetroots as above. Cool, peel and slice, then put in a salad bowl with the spinach and vinaigrette dressing. Lightly toast 4 slices of ciabatta or French bread on both sides under a preheated grill. Cut 100 g (3½ oz) goats' cheese into 4 slices and arrange on top of the toasted bread. Cook under the hot grill for a few minutes until the cheese has melted, then serve on a bed of salad. **Calories per serving 407**

green curry with straw mushrooms

Calories per serving **225**
Serves **4**
Preparation time **10 minutes**
Cooking time **10 minutes**

300 ml (½ pint) **coconut milk**,
  plus extra for drizzling
40 g (1½ oz) **green curry
  paste**
300 ml (½ pint) **vegetable
  stock**
2 **aubergines**, roughly
  chopped into large chunks
40 g (1½ oz) **soft brown
  sugar**
4 teaspoons **soy sauce**
25 g (1 oz) fresh **root ginger**,
  peeled and finely chopped
425 g (14 oz) can **straw
  mushrooms**, drained
50 g (2 oz) **green pepper**,
  cored, deseeded and
  thinly sliced
salt

Put most of the coconut milk and the curry paste in a saucepan over a medium heat and stir well. Pour in the stock, then add the aubergines, sugar, soy sauce, ginger and salt to taste.

Bring to the boil and cook, stirring, for 5 minutes. Add the mushrooms and green pepper, reduce the heat and cook for 2 minutes until piping hot.

Serve in bowls, drizzled with a little extra coconut milk.

For vegetable korma, heat 1 tablespoon vegetable oil in a large saucepan, add 1 finely diced onion, 3 bruised cardamom pods, 2 teaspoons each of ground cumin and ground coriander and ½ teaspoon turmeric and cook over a low heat for 5–6 minutes or until the onion is light golden. Add 1 deseeded and chopped green chilli, 1 crushed garlic clove and a thumb-sized piece of fresh root ginger, peeled and grated, and cook for 1 minute, then add 425 g (14 oz) prepared mixed vegetables, such as cauliflower, peppers, carrots and courgettes, and cook for a further 5 minutes. Remove the pan from the heat and stir through 200 ml (7 fl oz) yogurt and 2 tablespoons ground almonds. Serve sprinkled with chopped coriander. **Calories per serving 364**

sage & goats' cheese frittata

Calories per serving **232**
 (not including bread)
Serves **4**
Preparation time **10 minutes**
Cooking time **10 minutes**

25 g (1 oz) **butter**, plus extra
 if necessary
18 large **sage leaves**
50 g (2 oz) **soft goats'
 cheese**, crumbled
2 tablespoons **crème fraîche**
4 **eggs**
salt and **pepper**

Melt the butter in a nonstick frying pan. As soon as it stops foaming, add the sage leaves and fry over a medium-high heat, stirring, for 2–3 minutes until crisp and the butter turns golden brown. Take out 6 of the leaves and drain on kitchen paper. Transfer the remaining leaves and butter to a bowl.

Beat the goats' cheese and crème fraîche together in a separate bowl. Beat the eggs in another bowl, season with salt and pepper, then stir in the sage leaves with the butter.

Reheat the frying pan, adding a little extra butter if necessary. Pour in the egg mixture and dot over spoonfuls of the goats' cheese mixture. Cook over a medium heat for 4–5 minutes until the underside is set, then transfer to a preheated hot grill to brown the top lightly. Leave to cool slightly, then gently slide the frittata onto a serving plate. Garnish with the reserved sage leaves and serve with crusty bread, if liked.

For spinach & goats' cheese frittata, cook 175 g (6 oz) baby spinach leaves and 1 crushed garlic clove in the butter instead of the sage leaves for 2 minutes, or until the spinach has wilted. Stir into the beaten eggs at the second stage and continue with the recipe as above. **Calories per serving 240**

fennel & orange casserole

Calories per serving **232**
 (not including polenta)
Serves **4**
Preparation time **15 minutes**
Cooking time **about 50
 minutes**

2 **fennel bulbs**, trimmed
4 tablespoons **extra-virgin
 olive oil**
1 **onion**, chopped
2 **garlic cloves**, crushed
2 teaspoons chopped
 rosemary
100 ml (3½ fl oz) **Pernod**
400 g (13 oz) can **chopped
 tomatoes**
¼ teaspoon **saffron threads**
2 strips of **orange rind**
2 tablespoons chopped **fennel
 fronds**
salt and **pepper**

Cut the fennel lengthways into 5 mm (¼ inch) thick slices. Heat half the oil in a flameproof casserole, add the fennel slices, in batches, and cook over a medium heat for 3–4 minutes on each side until golden. Remove with a slotted spoon.

Heat the remaining oil in the casserole, add the onion, garlic, rosemary and salt and pepper and cook over a low heat, stirring frequently, for 5 minutes. Add the Pernod, bring to the boil and boil until reduced by half. Add the tomatoes, saffron and orange rind and stir well. Arrange the fennel slices over the top.

Bring the casserole to the boil, then cover with a tight-fitting lid and bake in a preheated oven, 180°C (350°F), Gas Mark 4, for 35 minutes until the fennel is tender. Stir in the fennel fronds and serve the casserole hot with some chargrilled polenta triangles, if liked.

For fennel gratin, prepare the fennel casserole as in the recipe above and transfer to a gratin dish. Combine 125 g (4 oz) fresh white breadcrumbs, 4 tablespoons grated Parmesan and 2 tablespoons chopped parsley. Scatter over the top of the fennel mixture and bake, uncovered, for 35 minutes. **Calories per serving 384**

spicy aubergine curry

Calories per serving **231**
Serves **4**
Preparation time **15 minutes,**
  plus cooling
Cooking time **20 minutes**

1 teaspoon **cumin seeds**
4 teaspoons **coriander seeds**
1 teaspoon **cayenne pepper**
2 **green chillies**, deseeded
  and sliced
½ teaspoon **turmeric**
4 **garlic cloves**, crushed
2.5 cm (1 inch) piece of **fresh**
  root ginger, peeled and
  grated
400 g (13 oz) can **reduced-fat**
  coconut milk
1 tablespoon **tamarind paste**
1 large **aubergine**, thinly
  sliced lengthways
salt and **pepper**
4 **mini plain naan breads**,
  to serve

Dry-fry the cumin and coriander seeds in a small, nonstick frying pan for a few minutes until aromatic and toasted. Leave to cool, then crush together.

Mix together the crushed seeds, cayenne pepper, chillies, turmeric, garlic, ginger and 300 ml (½ pint) warm water in a large saucepan and simmer for 10 minutes until thickened. Season with salt and pepper, then stir in the coconut milk and tamarind paste.

Arrange the aubergine slices on a foil-lined grill rack and brush the tops with some of the curry sauce. Cook under a preheated hot grill until golden.

Stir the grilled aubergine slices into the curry sauce. Serve hot with mini plain naan breads.

chermoula tofu & roasted veg

Calories per serving **241**
  (not including potatoes)
Serves **4**
Preparation time **15 minutes**
Cooking time **1 hour**

25 g (1 oz) **coriander**, finely
  chopped
3 **garlic cloves**, chopped
1 teaspoon **cumin seeds**,
  lightly crushed
finely grated rind of 1 **lemon**
½ teaspoon **dried crushed
  chillies**
4 tablespoons **olive oil**
250 g (8 oz) **tofu**
2 **red onions**, quartered
2 **courgettes**, thickly sliced
2 **red peppers**, deseeded
  and sliced
2 **yellow peppers**, deseeded
  and sliced
1 small **aubergine**, thickly
  sliced
salt

Mix the coriander, garlic, cumin, lemon rind and
chillies together with 1 tablespoon of the oil and
a little salt in a small bowl to make the chermoula.

Pat the tofu dry on kitchen paper and cut it in half.
Cut each half horizontally into thin slices. Spread the
chermoula generously over the slices.

Scatter the vegetables in a roasting tin and drizzle
with the remaining oil. Bake in a preheated oven,
200°C (400°F), Gas Mark 6, for about 45 minutes,
until lightly browned, turning the ingredients once or
twice during cooking.

Arrange the tofu slices over the vegetables, with
the side spread with the chermoula uppermost, and
bake for a further 10–15 minutes, until the tofu is
lightly coloured. Serve with lightly buttered new
potatoes, if liked.

stuffed mushrooms with tofu

Calories per serving **239**
Serves **4**
Preparation time **15 minutes**
Cooking time **18–20 minutes**

600 ml (1 pint) hot **vegetable stock**
4 large **portobello mushrooms**, stalks removed
2 tablespoons **olive oil**
75 g (3 oz) **red onion**, finely chopped
2 tablespoons **pine nuts**
250 g (8 oz) **tofu**, diced
½ teaspoon **cayenne pepper**
2 tablespoons chopped **basil**
50 g (2 oz) **Parmesan cheese**, finely grated
175 g (6 oz) **baby spinach leaves**
salt and **pepper**

Heat the stock in a pan over a medium heat, add the mushrooms, poach for 2–3 minutes, then remove and drain on kitchen paper.

Heat a little of the oil in a frying pan. Add the onion and fry gently until soft. Remove from the heat and allow to cool.

Dry-fry the pine nuts in a clean pan until golden-brown, remove from the heat, transfer to a bowl, then combine with the onion, tofu, cayenne pepper, basil and remaining oil. Season to taste with salt and pepper.

Sprinkle some grated Parmesan over each mushroom, then stuff the onion mixture into the mushrooms. Put them in a flameproof dish about 15 cm (6 inches) below a preheated medium grill for about 10 minutes, until heated through and the cheese has melted.

Scatter the spinach leaves on 4 plates and arrange a hot mushroom on top of each (the heat of the mushrooms will wilt the spinach).

For tofu & mushroom pasta, cook 300 g (10 oz) pasta in boiling water according to the instructions on the packet. Drain thoroughly. Meanwhile, slice 2 portobello mushrooms. Heat 1 tablespoon olive oil in a frying pan and fry the mushrooms with 40 g (1½ oz) chopped red onion. Add the mushrooms and onion to the pasta and add all the remaining ingredients above. Stir through 3 tablespoons double cream, warm gently and serve. **Calories per serving 486**

summer vegetable soup

Calories per serving **248**
Serves **2**
Preparation time **10 minutes**
Cooking time **15 minutes**

1 teaspoon **olive oil**
½ **leek**, finely sliced
½ large **potato**, chopped
200 g (7 oz) mixed summer
   vegetables, such as **peas**,
   asparagus, **broad beans**
   and **courgettes**
1 tablespoon chopped **mint**
450 ml (¾ pint) **vegetable**
   stock (see right for
   homemade)
1 tablespoon **crème fraîche**
salt (optional) and **black**
   pepper

Heat the oil in a medium saucepan, add the leek and potato and fry for 2–3 minutes until softened.

Add the vegetables to the pan with the mint and stock and bring to the boil. Reduce the heat and simmer for 10 minutes.

Transfer the soup to a blender or food processor and process until smooth. Return to the pan with the crème fraîche and season with salt (if liked) and pepper. Heat through and serve.

For homemade vegetable stock, heat 1 tablespoon olive oil in a large saucepan. Add 1 chopped onion, 1 chopped carrot, 4 chopped celery sticks and any available vegetable trimmings (such as celery stalks, onion skins and tomato skins) and fry for 2–3 minutes. Add 1 bouquet garni and season well with salt and pepper. Add 1.7 litres (2¾ pints) water and bring to the boil. Reduce the heat and simmer gently for 1½ hours. Strain. This makes about 1.2 litres (2 pints) of stock. **Calories per full amount 44**

malaysian coconut vegetables

Calories per serving **251**
Serves **4**
Preparation time **15 minutes,
plus soaking**
Cooking time **20 minutes**

125 g (4 oz) **broccoli florets**
125 g (4 oz) **green beans**, cut
into 2.5 cm (1 inch) lengths
1 **red pepper**, cored,
deseeded and sliced
125 g (4 oz) **courgettes**,
thinly sliced

Coconut sauce
25 g (1 oz) **tamarind pulp**
150 ml (¼ pint) **boiling water**
400 ml (14 fl oz) can **coconut
milk**
2 teaspoons **Thai green curry
paste**
1 teaspoon grated fresh
root ginger
1 **onion**, cut into small cubes
½ teaspoon **ground turmeric**
salt

Make the coconut sauce. Put the tamarind in a bowl.
Pour over the measurement water and leave to soak
for 30 minutes. Mash the tamarind in the water, then
push through a sieve set over another bowl, squashing
the tamarind so that you get as much of the pulp as
possible; discard the stringy bits and any seeds.

Take 2 tablespoons of the cream from the top of the
coconut milk and pour it into a wok or large frying pan.
Add the curry paste, ginger, onion and turmeric and
cook over a gentle heat, stirring, for 2–3 minutes. Stir
in the rest of the coconut milk and the tamarind water.
Bring to the boil, then reduce the heat to a simmer
and add a pinch of salt.

Add the broccoli to the coconut sauce and cook for
5 minutes, then add the green beans and red pepper.
Cook, stirring, for a further 5 minutes. Finally, stir in the
courgettes and cook gently for 1–2 minutes until just
tender. Serve immediately.

spring minestrone

Calories per serving **255**
  **(not including bread
  or toasts)**
Serves **6**
Preparation time **15 minutes**
Cooking time **55 minutes**

2 tablespoons **olive oil**
1 **onion**, thinly sliced
2 **carrots**, peeled and diced
2 **celery sticks**, diced
2 **garlic cloves**, peeled
1 **potato**, peeled and diced
125 g (4 oz) **peas** or **broad
  beans**, thawed if frozen
1 **courgette**, diced
125 g (4 oz) **green beans**,
  trimmed and cut into
  3.5 cm (1½ inch) pieces
125 g (4 oz) **plum tomatoes**,
  skinned and chopped
1.2 litres (2 pints) **vegetable
  stock**
75 g (3 oz) small **pasta
  shapes**
10 **basil leaves**, torn
salt and **pepper**

To serve
olive oil
grated **Parmesan cheese**

Heat the oil in a large, heavy-based saucepan over
a low heat. Add the onion, carrots, celery and garlic
and cook, stirring occasionally, for 10 minutes. Add
the potato, peas or broad beans, courgette and green
beans and cook, stirring frequently, for 2 minutes. Add
the tomatoes, season with salt and pepper and cook
for a further 2 minutes.

Pour in the stock and bring to the boil, then reduce the
heat and simmer gently for 20 minutes or until all the
vegetables are very tender.

Add the pasta and basil to the soup and cook, stirring
frequently, until the pasta is al dente. Season with salt
and pepper to taste.

Ladle into bowls, drizzle with olive oil and sprinkle with
the Parmesan. Serve with toasted country bread or
Parmesan toasts (see below).

For Parmesan toasts to serve as an accompaniment,
toast 6 slices of ciabatta on one side only under
a preheated medium grill. Brush the other side with
2–3 tablespoons olive oil and sprinkle with chilli flakes
and 2 tablespoons grated Parmesan cheese, then
cook under the preheated grill until golden and crisp.
Calories per serving 180

chickpea & chilli salad

Calories per serving **297**
Serves **4**
Preparation time **10 minutes,
plus standing**

2 x 400 g (13 oz) cans
  chickpeas, rinsed and
  drained
2 **plum tomatoes**, roughly
  chopped
4 **spring onions**, thinly sliced
1 fresh **red chilli**, deseeded
  and thinly sliced
4 tablespoons roughly
  chopped **coriander leaves**
2 full-sized **pitta breads**,
  grilled and cut into thin
  fingers, to serve

Lemon dressing
2 tablespoons **lemon juice**
1 **garlic clove**, crushed
2 tablespoons **olive oil**
salt and **pepper**

Combine all the salad ingredients in a shallow bowl. Put all the dressing ingredients in a screw-top jar, season to taste with salt and pepper, and shake well. Pour over the salad and toss well to coat all the ingredients.

Cover the salad and leave to stand at room temperature for about 10 minutes to allow the flavours to mingle. Serve with the grilled pitta bread fingers.

For white bean & sun-dried tomato salad, combine 2 x 400 g (13 oz) cans cannellini beans, rinsed and drained, 125 g (4 oz) sun-dried tomatoes in oil, drained and roughly chopped, 1 tablespoon chopped and pitted black olives, 2 teaspoons rinsed and drained capers and 2 teaspoons chopped thyme leaves. Toss in the lemon dressing and leave to stand as above, then serve with toasted slices of ciabatta. **Calories per serving 454**

garlicky choi sum

Calories per serving **91**
Serves **4**
Preparation time **5 minutes**
Cooking time **5 minutes**

500 g (1 lb) **choi sum**
2 tablespoons **groundnut oil**
3 **garlic cloves**, sliced
1 teaspoon **salt**
2 tablespoons **Chinese rice wine** or **dry sherry**
1 teaspoon **sesame oil**

Trim 5 cm (2 inches) from the ends of the choi sum, then cut it into 5 cm (2 inch) lengths. Wash thoroughly.

Heat the oil in a wok over a high heat until the oil starts to shimmer. Add the garlic and salt and stir-fry for 15 seconds, then tip in the choi sum and stir-fry for 1 minute.

Add the rice wine and 150 ml (½ pint) water and stir-fry for about 2–3 minutes, until the choi sum is tender and most of the liquid has evaporated. Stir in the sesame oil and serve immediately.

For pak choi with water chestnuts & garlic, follow the recipe as above, replacing the choi sum with 500 g (1 lb) pak choi, cut into 5 cm (2 inch) lengths, and 4 halved tinned water chestnuts. **Calories per serving 97**

watermelon, fennel & feta salad

Calories per serving **266**
Serves **4**
Preparation time **10 minutes**
Cooking time **2 minutes**

350 g (11½ oz) **fresh** or
  frozen shelled broad beans
1 large **fennel bulb**
250 g (8 oz) **watermelon**
  flesh, diced
125 g (4 oz) **feta cheese**,
  crumbled
salt and **pepper**

Dressing
3 tablespoons **extra-virgin**
  olive oil
1 tablespoon **lemon juice**
1 teaspoon **clear honey**
1 teaspoon **pomegranate**
  syrup

Cook the beans in a large saucepan of lightly salted boiling water for 2 minutes. Drain and immediately refresh under cold water. Pat dry with kitchen paper, then peel off and discard the tough outer skins. Put the beans in a bowl.

Trim the fennel bulb. Cut in half, then crossways into wafer-thin slices. Add to the beans with the watermelon and feta.

Whisk all the dressing ingredients together in a small bowl and season with salt and pepper. Pour over the salad, toss well and serve.

For fennel, orange & parsley salad, very thinly slice a large fennel bulb into a bowl and add ½ bunch of parsley, 2 tablespoons drained baby capers and 1 peeled and segmented orange. Add the juice of ½ lemon, 1 tablespoon orange juice and a good spoonful of extra-virgin olive oil. Season with salt and pepper and mix well to combine. **Calories per serving 63**

spicy apple & potato soup

Calories per serving **266**
Serves **4**
Preparation time **15 minutes**
Cooking time **30 minutes**

50 g (2 oz) **butter**
1 small **onion**, chopped
2 **dessert apples**, peeled,
  cored and sliced
pinch of **cayenne pepper**
  (or to taste), plus extra for
  sprinkling
600 ml (1 pint) **vegetable
  stock**
300 g (10 oz) **floury
  potatoes**, sliced
300 ml (½ pint) **hot milk**
salt

Apple garnish
15 g (½ oz) **butter**
½–1 **dessert apple**, peeled,
  cored and diced

Melt the butter in a large heavy-based saucepan over a medium heat. Add the onion and cook for 5 minutes or until softened. Add the apples and cayenne pepper and cook, stirring, for a further 2 minutes.

Pour in the stock, then add the potatoes. Bring to the boil, then reduce the heat and simmer gently for 15–18 minutes until the apples and potatoes are very tender.

Blend the soup in batches in a blender or food processor until very smooth, then transfer to a clean saucepan. Reheat gently and stir in the hot milk. Taste and adjust the seasoning if necessary.

Make the apple garnish, meanwhile. Melt the butter in a small frying pan, add the diced apple and cook over a high heat until crisp.

Serve the soup in warmed bowls, garnishing each portion with some diced apple and a sprinkling of cayenne pepper.

For spicy apple & parsnip soup, fry the onion and apples as above, omitting the cayenne pepper. Add ½ teaspoon ground turmeric and 1 teaspoon ground coriander and stir through to coat the apple and onion mixture in the spices. Pour in 600 ml (1 pint) vegetable stock, then add 300 g (10 oz) diced parsnips instead of the potatoes. Season with salt and black pepper. Continue the recipe as above. **Calories per serving 257**

italian broccoli & egg salad

Calories per serving **211**
  (not including bread)
Serves **4**
Preparation time **10 minutes**
Cooking time **8 minutes**

4 eggs
300 g (10 oz) **broccoli**
2 small **leeks**, about 300 g
  (10 oz) in total
sprigs of **tarragon,** to garnish
  (optional)

Dressing
4 tablespoons **lemon juice**
2 tablespoons **olive oil**
2 teaspoons **clear honey**
1 tablespoon **capers**, rinsed
  and drained
2 tablespoons chopped
  tarragon
salt and **pepper**

Half-fill the base of a steamer with water, add the eggs and bring to the boil. Cover with the steamer top and simmer for 8 minutes or until hard-boiled.

Meanwhile, cut the broccoli into florets and thickly slice the stems. Trim, slit and wash the leeks and cut them into thick slices. Add the broccoli to the top of the steamer and cook for 3 minutes, then add the leeks and cook for a further 2 minutes.

Make the dressing by mixing together the lemon juice, oil, honey, capers and tarragon in a salad bowl. Season to taste with salt and pepper.

Crack the eggs, cool them quickly under cold running water and remove the shells. Roughly chop the eggs.

Add the broccoli and leeks to the dressing, toss together and add the chopped eggs. Garnish with sprigs of tarragon and serve warm with thickly sliced wholemeal bread, if liked.

aubergine, tomato & feta rolls

Calories per serving **270**
Serves **4**
Preparation time **15 minutes**
Cooking time **about**
6 minutes

2 **aubergines**
3 tablespoons **olive oil**
125 g (4 oz) **feta cheese,**
  roughly diced
12 **sun-dried tomatoes**
  in oil, drained
15–20 **basil leaves**
salt and **pepper**

Trim the ends of the aubergines, then cut a thin slice lengthways from either side of each; discard these slices, which should be mainly skin. Cut each aubergine lengthways into 4 slices. Heat the grill on the hottest setting or heat a griddle pan until very hot.

Brush both sides of the aubergine slices with the oil, then cook under the grill or in the griddle pan for 3 minutes on each side or until browned and softened.

Lay the aubergine slices on a board and divide the feta, tomatoes and basil leaves between them. Season well with salt and pepper.

Roll up each slice from the short end and secure with a cocktail stick. Arrange on serving plates and serve immediately, or cover and set aside in a cool place, but not the refrigerator, and serve at room temperature when required.

For courgette & mozzarella rolls, use 3–4 large courgettes, then trim the ends and sides as for the aubergines. Cut each courgette lengthways into 3 slices, depending on their size, brush with oil and cook under the grill or in a griddle pan as for the aubergines until browned and softened. Spread the courgette slices with 2 tablespoons red pesto, then top with 125 g (4 oz) diced mozzarella cheese and the basil leaves. Roll up and serve as above. **Calories per serving 245**

fennel soup with olive gremolata

Calories per serving **218**
Serves **4**
Preparation time **20 minutes**
Cooking time **40 minutes**

75 ml (3 fl oz) **extra-virgin olive oil**
3 **spring onions**, chopped
250 g (8 oz) **fennel**, trimmed, cored and thinly sliced, reserving any green fronds for the gremolata and chopping them finely
1 **potato**, diced
finely grated rind and juice of 1 **lemon**
750 ml (1¼ pints) **vegetable stock**
salt and **pepper**

Gremolata
1 small **garlic clove**, finely chopped
finely grated rind of 1 **lemon**
4 tablespoons chopped **parsley**
16 **black olives**, pitted and chopped

Heat the oil in a large saucepan, add the spring onions and cook for 5–10 minutes until beginning to soften. Add the fennel, potato and lemon rind and cook for 5 minutes until the fennel begins to soften. Pour in the stock and bring to the boil. Turn down the heat, cover and simmer for about 25 minutes or until the ingredients are tender.

Make the gremolata. Mix together the garlic, lemon rind, chopped fennel fronds and parsley, then stir the chopped olives into the herb mixture. Cover and chill.

Liquidize the soup and pass it through a sieve to remove any strings of fennel. The soup should not be too thick, so add more stock if necessary. Return it to the rinsed pan. Taste and season well with salt, pepper and plenty of lemon juice. Pour into warmed bowls and sprinkle each serving with a portion of the gremolata.

For fennel & almond soup with orange & olive gremolata, add 75 g (3 oz) blanched almonds to the pan with the onions. Complete the recipe as above, omitting the potato. Make the gremolata as above, replacing the lemon with the finely grated rind of 1 orange. **Calories per serving 293**

squash, carrot & mango tagine

Calories per serving **232**
  (not including couscous)
Serves **4**
Preparation time **15 minutes**
Cooking time **35–40 minutes**

2 tablespoons **olive oil**
1 large **onion**, cut into large
  chunks
3 **garlic cloves**, finely chopped
1 **butternut squash**, about
  875 g (1¾ lb) in total,
  peeled, deseeded and cubed
2 small **carrots**, peeled and
  cut into thick batons
a 1 cm (½ inch) **cinnamon
  stick**
½ teaspoon **turmeric**
¼ teaspoon **cayenne pepper**
  (optional)
½ teaspoon **ground cumin**
1 teaspoon **paprika**
pinch of **saffron threads**
1 tablespoon **tomato purée**
750 ml (1¼ pints) hot
  vegetable stock
1 **mango**, peeled, stoned
  and cut into 2.5 cm (1 inch)
  chunks
salt and **pepper**
2 tablespoons chopped
  coriander, to garnish

Heat the oil in a large, heavy-based saucepan over
a medium heat, add the onion and cook for 5 minutes
or until beginning to soften. Add the garlic, butternut
squash, carrots and spices and fry gently for a further
5 minutes.

Stir in the tomato purée, then pour in the stock and
season with salt and pepper to taste. Cover and simmer
gently for 20–25 minutes or until the vegetables are
tender. Stir in the mango and simmer gently for a further
5 minutes.

Ladle the tagine into serving bowls, sprinkle with the
coriander and serve with steamed couscous, if liked.

For spicy squash & carrot soup, make the tagine as
above, adding an extra 250 ml (8 fl oz) vegetable stock.
Once the vegetables are tender, place in a blender
or food processor and blend until smooth. Ladle into
bowls and serve scattered with the chopped coriander.
Calories per serving 237

stir-fried tofu with basil & chilli

Calories per serving **273**
Serves **4**
Preparation time **20 minutes**
Cooking time **6 minutes**

2 tablespoons **sunflower oil**
350 g (11½ oz) **firm tofu**, cubed
5 cm (2 inch) piece of fresh **root ginger**, shredded
2 **garlic cloves,** chopped
250 g (8 oz) **broccoli**, trimmed
250 g (8 oz) **sugar snap peas**, trimmed
150 ml (¼ pint) **vegetable stock**
2 tablespoons **sweet chilli sauce**
1 tablespoon **light soy sauce**
1 tablespoon **dark soy sauce**
1 tablespoon **lime juice**
2 teaspoons **soft light brown sugar**
handful of **Thai basil leaves**

Heat half the oil in a wok or deep frying pan until smoking, then add the tofu and stir-fry for 2–3 minutes until golden all over. Remove with a slotted spoon.

Add the remaining oil to the pan, add the ginger and garlic and stir-fry for 10 seconds, then add the broccoli and sugar snap peas and stir-fry for 1 minute.

Return the tofu to the pan and add the stock, chilli sauce, soy sauces, lime juice and sugar. Cook for 1 minute until the vegetables are cooked but still crisp. Add the basil leaves and stir well.

For tofu & vegetables in oyster sauce, cook the tofu and vegetables as in the recipe above. Return the tofu to the pan and add 50 ml (2 fl oz) water, cook for 1 minute, then add 75 ml (3 fl oz) oyster sauce and heat through for a further minute. Omit the basil and garnish with chopped fresh coriander. **Calories per serving 244**

pumpkin soup with olive salsa

Calories per serving **235**
Serves **6**
Preparation time **20 minutes**
Cooking time **40 minutes**

4 tablespoons **olive oil**
1 large **onion**, chopped
2 **garlic cloves,** crushed
1 tablespoon chopped **sage**
1 kg (2 lb) peeled, deseeded
  pumpkin, cubed
400 g (13 oz) can **cannellini**
  or **haricot beans**, rinsed
  and drained
1 litre (1¾ pints) **vegetable
  stock**
salt and **pepper**

For the olive salsa
100 g (3½ oz) **pitted black
  olives**
3 tablespoons **extra-virgin
  olive oil**
grated rind of 1 **lemon**
2 tablespoons chopped
  parsley

Heat the oil in a saucepan, add the onion, garlic and
sage and cook over a low heat, stirring frequently, for
5 minutes. Add the pumpkin and beans and stir well,
then add the stock and a little salt and pepper.

Bring to the boil, then reduce the heat, cover and
simmer gently for 30 minutes until the pumpkin is
tender. Transfer the soup to a blender or food processor
and process until smooth. Return to the pan, adjust the
seasoning and heat through.

Meanwhile, make the salsa. Chop the olives and mix
with the oil, lemon rind, parsley and salt and pepper
in a bowl.

Serve the soup in warmed bowls, topped with
spoonfuls of the salsa.

For roasted butternut squash soup, use 1 kg (2 lb)
butternut squash instead of pumpkin. Toss the cubes
of butternut squash with 1 tablespoon olive oil and
roast in a preheated oven, 200°C (400°F), Gas Mark
6, for 30 minutes until golden and tender. Continue
with the recipe as above, but cook the soup for just
15 minutes. **Calories per serving 291**

spicy lentils & chickpeas

Calories per serving **276**
  **(not including rice
  and yogurt)**
Serves **4**
Preparation time **15 minutes**
Cooking time **35 minutes**

1 tablespoon **groundnut oil**
1 **onion**, finely chopped
2 **garlic cloves**, thinly sliced
2 **celery sticks**, diced
1 **green pepper**, cored,
  deseeded and chopped
150 g (5 oz) **red split lentils**,
  rinsed
2 teaspoons **garam masala**
1 teaspoon **cumin seeds**
½ teaspoon **hot chilli powder**
1 teaspoon **ground coriander**
2 tablespoons **tomato purée**
750 ml (1¼ pints) hot
  vegetable stock
400 g (13 oz) can **chickpeas,**
  rinsed and drained
salt and **pepper**
2 tablespoons chopped
  coriander, to garnish

Heat the oil in a heavy-based saucepan over a medium
heat, add the onion, garlic, celery and green pepper
and fry gently for 10–12 minutes or until softened
and beginning to colour.

Stir in the lentils and spices and cook for 2–3 minutes,
stirring frequently. Add the tomato purée, stock and
chickpeas and bring to the boil. Reduce the heat, cover
and simmer gently for about 20 minutes or until the
lentils collapse. Season with salt and pepper to taste.

Ladle into bowls and sprinkle with the coriander. Serve
immediately with boiled brown rice and cooling, spiced
yogurt (see below), if liked.

For cooling, spiced yogurt to serve as an
accompaniment, mix together 200 g (7 oz) fat-free
natural yogurt, 2 tablespoons lemon juice and
½ teaspoon garam masala in a small bowl. Fold
in ½ small, deseeded and grated cucumber, then
season with salt and pepper to taste. Serve sprinkled
with 1 tablespoon chopped coriander. **Calories per
serving 36**

mushroom stroganoff

Calories per serving **239**
Serves **4**
Preparation time **10 minutes**
Cooking time **10 minutes**

1 tablespoon **butter**
2 tablespoons **olive oil**
1 **onion**, thinly sliced
4 **garlic cloves**, finely chopped
500 g (1 lb) **chestnut mushrooms**, sliced
2 tablespoons **wholegrain mustard**
250 ml (8 fl oz) **half-fat crème fraîche**
salt and **pepper**
3 tablespoons chopped **parsley**, to garnish

Melt the butter with the oil in a large frying pan, add the onion and garlic and cook until soft and starting to brown.

Add the mushrooms to the pan and cook until soft and starting to brown. Stir in the mustard and crème fraîche and just heat through. Season to taste with salt and pepper, then serve immediately, garnished with the chopped parsley.

For mushroom soup with garlic croûtons, while the mushrooms are cooking, remove the crusts from 2 thick slices of day-old white bread and rub with 2 halved garlic cloves. Cut the bread into cubes. Fry the cubes of bread in a little vegetable oil in a frying pan, turning constantly, for 5 minutes or until browned all over and crisp. Drain on kitchen paper. After adding the mustard and crème fraîche to the mushroom mixture as above, add 400 ml (14 fl oz) hot vegetable stock, then purée the mixture in a blender or food processor until smooth. Serve in warmed bowls, topped with the croûtons and garnished with the chopped parsley.
Calories per serving 273

griddled vegetable platter

Calories per serving **285**
(not including bread)
Serves **4**
Preparation time **10 minutes**,
plus marinating
Cooking time **20 minutes**

2 **courgettes**, sliced
lengthways into 5 mm
(¼ inch) thick slices
1 **aubergine**, sliced
lengthways into 5 mm
(¼ inch) thick slices
1 **yellow pepper**, cored,
deseeded and cut into
2.5 cm (1 inch) thick slices
1 **red pepper**, cored,
deseeded and cut into
2.5 cm (1 inch) thick slices
100 ml (3½ fl oz) **extra-virgin
olive oil**
2 **garlic cloves**, crushed
large pinch of **crushed dried
chillies**
handful of small **mint** and/or
basil leaves
salt

Toss all the prepared vegetables in 2 tablespoons of the oil until well coated.

Heat a ridged griddle pan over a high heat until smoking hot. Add the courgettes and aubergine in batches and cook for 2–3 minutes on each side. Transfer to a bowl and toss with the remaining oil, the garlic and crushed dried chillies. Set aside.

Add the peppers in batches to the reheated griddle pan and cook for 3–4 minutes on each side, then combine with the courgettes and aubergine. Season with salt and toss in the herbs.

Cover and leave to marinate at room temperature for 30 minutes. Serve with slices of country bread, if liked.

For griddled courgettes with lemon, mint & Parmesan, omit the peppers and aubergine and slice 4 large courgettes lengthways into 5 mm (¼ inch) slices, toss with oil and then griddle as above. Transfer to a bowl and toss with the remaining oil, the garlic and crushed chillies as above, adding a handful of small mint leaves, torn, but not the basil. Leave to marinate as above, then serve with a generous topping of Parmesan cheese shavings and the finely grated rind of ½ lemon. **Calories per serving 326**

home baked beans

Calories per serving **235**
  (not including toast)
Serves **4**
Preparation time **10 minutes**
Cooking time **about 2 hours**

2 x 400 g (13 oz) cans **borlotti
  beans**, rinsed and drained
1 **garlic clove**, crushed
1 **onion**, finely chopped
450 ml (¾ pint) **vegetable
  stock**
300 ml (½ pint) **passata**
  (sieved tomatoes)
2 tablespoons **molasses** or
  black treacle
2 tablespoons **tomato purée**
2 tablespoons **soft dark
  brown sugar**
1 tablespoon **Dijon mustard**
1 tablespoon **red wine
  vinegar**
salt and **pepper**

Put all the ingredients in a flameproof casserole with a little salt and pepper. Cover and bring slowly to the boil.

Bake in a preheated oven, 160°C (325°F), Gas Mark 3, for 1½ hours. Remove the lid and bake for a further 30 minutes until the sauce is syrupy. Serve with hot buttered toast, if liked.

For home baked beans with jacket potatoes, scrub 4 Desiree or King Edward potatoes, about 200 g (7 oz) each, then bake in a preheated oven, 200°C (400°F), Gas Mark 6, for about 1 hour until cooked through. Cut lengthways in half, season with salt and pepper and spoon over the beans. Grate over a little Cheddar cheese before serving. The home baked beans are even better made a day ahead and heated through before serving. **Calories per serving 487**

chicory & baby cos salad

Calories per serving **288**
Serves **4**
Preparation time **10 minutes**

2 **chicory heads, white and
    red** if possible, about 175 g
    (6 oz) in total
3 baby **cos lettuce hearts**

Dressing
50 g (2 oz) **Gorgonzola
    cheese**
1 tablespoon **Worcestershire
    sauce**
2 tablespoons **mayonnaise**
2 tablespoons **soured cream**
3 tablespoons **olive oil**
1 tablespoon **white wine
    vinegar**
2 tablespoons **lemon juice**
salt and **pepper**

Slice the base of the chicory heads and the lettuces
and carefully remove the individual leaves. Put the
leaves in a large salad bowl.

Make the dressing by whisking together all the
ingredients. Season to taste with salt and pepper.

Add the dressing to the lettuce and chicory leaves, toss
briefly to mix and serve.

For Gorgonzola, pecan & pear salad, prepare the
salad leaves as above. Add 50 g (2 oz) toasted pecan
nuts and 1 finely sliced pear to the chicory and lettuce
leaves. Toss well. Whisk the dressing ingredients as
above, toss through the salad and serve immediately.
Calories per serving 389

carrot & cashew nut salad

Calories per serving **253**
Serves **4**
Preparation time **10 minutes**
Cooking time **6–10 minutes**

75 g (3 oz) **unsalted
cashew nuts**
2 tablespoons **black
mustard seeds**
500 g (1 lb) **carrots**, peeled
and coarsely grated
1 **red pepper**, cored,
deseeded and thinly sliced
3 tablespoons chopped
chervil
2 **spring onions**, finely sliced

Dressing
2 tablespoons **avocado oil**
2 tablespoons **raspberry
vinegar**
1 tablespoon **wholegrain
mustard**
pinch of **sugar**
salt and **pepper**

Heat a nonstick frying pan over a medium-low heat
and dry-fry the cashew nuts for 5–8 minutes, stirring
frequently, or until golden brown and toasted. Tip onto
a small plate and leave to cool. Add the mustard seeds
to the pan and dry-fry for 1–2 minutes or until they
start to pop.

Mix together the mustard seeds, carrots, red pepper,
chervil and spring onions in a large bowl.

Whisk together all the dressing ingredients in a small
bowl, then pour onto the grated carrot salad. Mix
thoroughly to coat and heap into serving bowls. Chop
the cashew nuts coarsely and scatter over the salad.
Serve immediately.

For carrot & celeriac coleslaw, mix together 300 g
(10 oz) grated carrot and 200 g (7 oz) coarsely grated
celeriac with the mustard seeds, chervil, spring onions
and dressing, omitting the red pepper. Replace the
cashew nuts with 75 g (3 oz) chopped walnuts and
serve as above. **Calories per serving 253**

poached eggs & spinach

Calories per serving **291**
Serves **4**
Preparation time **5 minutes**
Cooking time **8–10 minutes**

4 strips of **cherry tomatoes**
 on the vine, about 6 tomatoes
 on each
2 tablespoons **balsamic syrup**
 or **glaze**
1 small bunch of **basil leaves**
1 tablespoon **distilled vinegar**
4 large **eggs**
4 thick slices of **wholemeal**
 bread
reduced-fat butter, to spread
 (optional)
100 g (3½ oz) **baby spinach**
 leaves
salt and **pepper**

Lay the cherry tomato vines in an ovenproof dish, drizzle with the balsamic syrup or glaze, scatter with the basil leaves and season with salt and pepper. Place in a preheated oven, 180°C (350°F), Gas Mark 4, for 8–10 minutes or until the tomatoes begin to collapse.

Meanwhile, bring a large saucepan of water to a gentle simmer, add the vinegar and stir with a large spoon to create a swirl. Carefully break 2 eggs into the water and cook for 3 minutes. Remove with a slotted spoon and keep warm. Repeat with the remaining two eggs.

Toast the wholemeal bread and butter lightly, if liked.

Heap the spinach onto serving plates and top each plate with a poached egg. Arrange the vine tomatoes on the plates, drizzled with any cooking juices. Serve immediately with the wholemeal toast, cut into fingers.

For spinach, egg & cress salad, gently lower the unshelled eggs into a saucepan of simmering water. Cook for 7–8 minutes, then cool quickly under cold running water. Shell the eggs and slice thickly. Arrange the egg slices over the spinach leaves and halved cherry tomatoes. Scatter with 20 g (¾ oz) salad cress and serve with a little olive oil and balsamic syrup. **Calories per serving 241**

winter vegetable & beer broth

Calories per serving **237**
(**not including bread**)
Serves **6**
Preparation time **20 minutes**
Cooking time **50–55 minutes**

4 tablespoons **olive oil**
1 **onion**, chopped
2 **garlic cloves**, crushed
1 tablespoon chopped
rosemary
2 **carrots**, diced
250 g (8 oz) **parsnips**, diced
250 g (8 oz) **swede**, diced
100 g (3½ oz) **pearl barley**
600 ml (1 pint) **beer** or **lager**
1 litre (1¾ pints) **vegetable stock**
2 tablespoons chopped
parsley
salt and **pepper**

Heat the oil in a large saucepan, add the onion, garlic, rosemary, carrots, parsnips and swede and cook over a low heat, stirring frequently, for 10 minutes.

Stir in the pearl barley, beer or lager, stock and salt and pepper and bring to the boil. Reduce the heat, cover and simmer gently for 40–45 minutes until the barley and vegetables are tender. Stir in the parsley and adjust the seasoning. Serve in warmed bowls with crusty bread, if liked.

For vegetable & rice soup, omit the beer and increase the stock to 1.5 litres (2½ pints). Replace the pearl barley with an equal quantity of risotto rice. Use 250 g (8 oz) celeriac instead of the parsnips. Continue the recipe as above. Serve the soup garnished with some more chopped parsley and cracked black pepper. **Calories per serving 195**

indian spiced pumpkin wedges

Calories per serving **292**
Serves **4**
Preparation time **15 minutes,**
    plus cooling
Cooking time **15–20 minutes**

1 kg (2 lb) **pumpkin** or
    butternut squash
1 teaspoon **cumin seeds**
1 teaspoon **coriander seeds**
2 **cardamom pods**
3 tablespoons **sunflower oil**
1 teaspoon **caster sugar** or
    mango chutney

Coconut pesto
25 g (1 oz) fresh **coriander**
    leaves
1 **garlic clove**, crushed
1 **green chilli**, deseeded and
    chopped
pinch of **caster sugar**
1 tablespoon **pistachio nuts**,
    roughly chopped
6 tablespoons **coconut cream**
1 tablespoon **lime juice**
salt and **pepper**

Cut the pumpkin or butternut squash into thin wedges about 1 cm (½ inch) thick, discarding the seeds and fibres, and put in a large dish.

Heat a heavy-based frying pan until hot, add the whole spices and dry-fry over a medium heat, stirring, until browned. Leave to cool, then grind to a powder in a spice grinder or in a mortar with a pestle. Mix the ground spices with the oil and sugar or mango chutney in a small bowl, then add to the pumpkin wedges and toss well to coat.

Cook the pumpkin or squash wedges under a preheated hot grill, or over a preheated hot gas barbecue or the hot coals of a charcoal barbecue, for 6–8 minutes on each side until charred and tender.

Meanwhile, make the pesto. Put the coriander leaves, garlic, chilli, sugar and pistachio nuts in a food processor and process until fairly finely ground and blended. Season with salt and pepper. Add the coconut cream and lime juice and process again. Transfer to a serving bowl. Serve the wedges hot with the coconut pesto.

For Indian-spiced sweet potato wedges, cook 4 scrubbed sweet potatoes, 250 g (8 oz) each, in a large saucepan of simmering water for 15 minutes, or until just tender, then drain. When cool enough to handle, slice into large wedges. Toss with the spice and oil mixture and grill or barbecue, as above, for about 6 minutes, turning frequently, until browned. Serve hot with the coconut pesto. **Calories per serving 419**

138

porridge with prune compote

Calories per serving **259**
Serves **8**
Preparation time **5 minutes**
Cooking time **about
  20 minutes**

1 litre (1¾ pints) **skimmed
  or semi-skimmed milk**
1 teaspoon **vanilla extract**
pinch of **ground cinnamon**
pinch of **salt**
200 g (7 oz) **porridge oats**
3 tablespoons **flaked
  almonds**, toasted

Compote
250 g (8 oz) **ready-to-eat
  dried Agen prunes**
125 ml (4 fl oz) **apple juice**
1 small **cinnamon stick**
1 **clove**
1 tablespoon **runny honey**
1 unpeeled **orange quarter**

Place all the compote ingredients in a small saucepan over a medium heat. Simmer gently for 10–12 minutes or until softened and slightly sticky. Leave to cool. (The compote can be prepared in advance and chilled.)

Put the milk, 500 ml (17 fl oz) water, vanilla extract, cinnamon and salt in a large saucepan over a medium heat and bring slowly to the boil. Stir in the oats, then reduce the heat and simmer gently, stirring occasionally, for 8–10 minutes until creamy and tender.

Spoon the porridge into warmed bowls, scatter with the almonds and serve with the prune compote.

For sweet quinoa porridge with banana & dates,
put 250 g (8 oz) quinoa in a saucepan with the milk, 1 tablespoon agave nectar or honey and 2–3 cardamom pods. Simmer gently for 12–15 minutes or until the quinoa is cooked and the desired consistency is reached. Serve in bowls topped with a dollop of fat-free natural yogurt, 100 g (3½ oz) chopped dates and freshly sliced banana. **Calories per serving 259**

recipes under 400 calories

baked tortillas with hummus

Calories per serving **312**
Serves **4**
Preparation time **5 minutes**
Cooking time **10–12 minutes**

4 small **soft flour tortillas**
1 tablespoon **olive oil**

Hummus
400 g (13 oz) can **chickpeas**,
  rinsed and drained
1 **garlic clove**, chopped
4 tablespoons **Greek-style
  yogurt**
2 tablespoons **lemon juice**
1 small bunch fresh **coriander**,
  chopped
salt and **pepper**
paprika, for sprinkling

Make the hummus first. Put the chickpeas in a bowl and mash with a fork to break them up. Add the garlic, yogurt, lemon juice and coriander and season with salt and pepper. Mix together. Alternatively, put all the ingredients, except the coriander, in a blender or food processor and blend to a coarse purée. Add the coriander and whiz briefly until mixed through. Put the hummus in a serving bowl or dish and sprinkle with a little paprika.

Cut each tortilla into 8 triangles, put on a baking sheet and brush with a little oil. Bake in a preheated oven, 200°C (400°F), Gas Mark 6, for 10–12 minutes until golden and crisp. Remove from the oven.

Serve the tortilla triangles with the hummus for dipping or spreading on top.

For baked tortillas with broad bean hummus, cook 400 g (13 oz) frozen broad beans in boiling water for 4–5 minutes until tender. Drain, then mash or purée with the garlic, yogurt, lemon juice, salt and pepper as above. Mix in 3 tablespoons chopped mint leaves, 1 chopped deseeded fresh green chilli and 1 teaspoon ground cumin instead of the fresh coriander.
Calories per serving 324

roasted summer vegetables

Calories per serving **399**
Serves **4**
Preparation time **15 minutes**
Cooking time **45–50 minutes**

1 **red pepper**, cored,
   deseeded and thickly sliced
1 **yellow pepper**, cored,
   deseeded and thickly sliced
1 **aubergine**, cut into chunks
2 **yellow** or **green courgettes**,
   cut into chunks
1 **red onion**, cut into wedges
6 **garlic cloves**
2 tablespoons **extra-virgin**
   olive oil or **rapeseed oil**
4–5 **thyme sprigs**
150 g (5 oz) **yellow** and
   red baby plum tomatoes
150 g (5 oz) **hazelnuts**
125 g (4 oz) **rocket leaves**
2 tablespoons **raspberry**
   or **balsamic vinegar**
salt and **pepper**
handful of **mustard cress**,
   to garnish (optional)

Toss all the vegetables, except the tomatoes, and garlic in a large bowl with the oil. Season with a little salt and pepper and add the thyme. Tip into a large roasting tin and place in a preheated oven, 190°C (375°F), Gas Mark 5, for 40–45 minutes or until the vegetables are tender. Add the tomatoes and return to the oven for a further 5 minutes or until the tomatoes are just softened and beginning to burst.

Tip the hazelnuts into a small roasting tin, meanwhile, and place in the oven for about 10–12 minutes or until golden and the skin is peeling away. Leave to cool, then remove the excess skin and crush lightly.

Toss the rocket leaves gently with the mixed, roasted vegetables and heap onto large plates. Scatter over the crushed hazelnuts and drizzle with the vinegar. Scatter over the mustard cress, if using, and serve immediately.

For roasted vegetable pasta sauce, roast the vegetables as above, then tip into a large saucepan with the rest of the vegetables, 500 ml (17 fl oz) passata and 150 ml (¼ pint) vegetable stock. Bring to the boil, then reduce the heat and simmer gently for 20 minutes. Remove from the heat and use a hand-held blender to blend until smooth. Season with salt and pepper to taste and serve with hot pasta (150 g/5 oz per serving). Alternatively, stir in an extra 250 ml (8 fl oz) vegetable stock to make soup. **Calories per serving sauce only 182 (with pasta 421)**

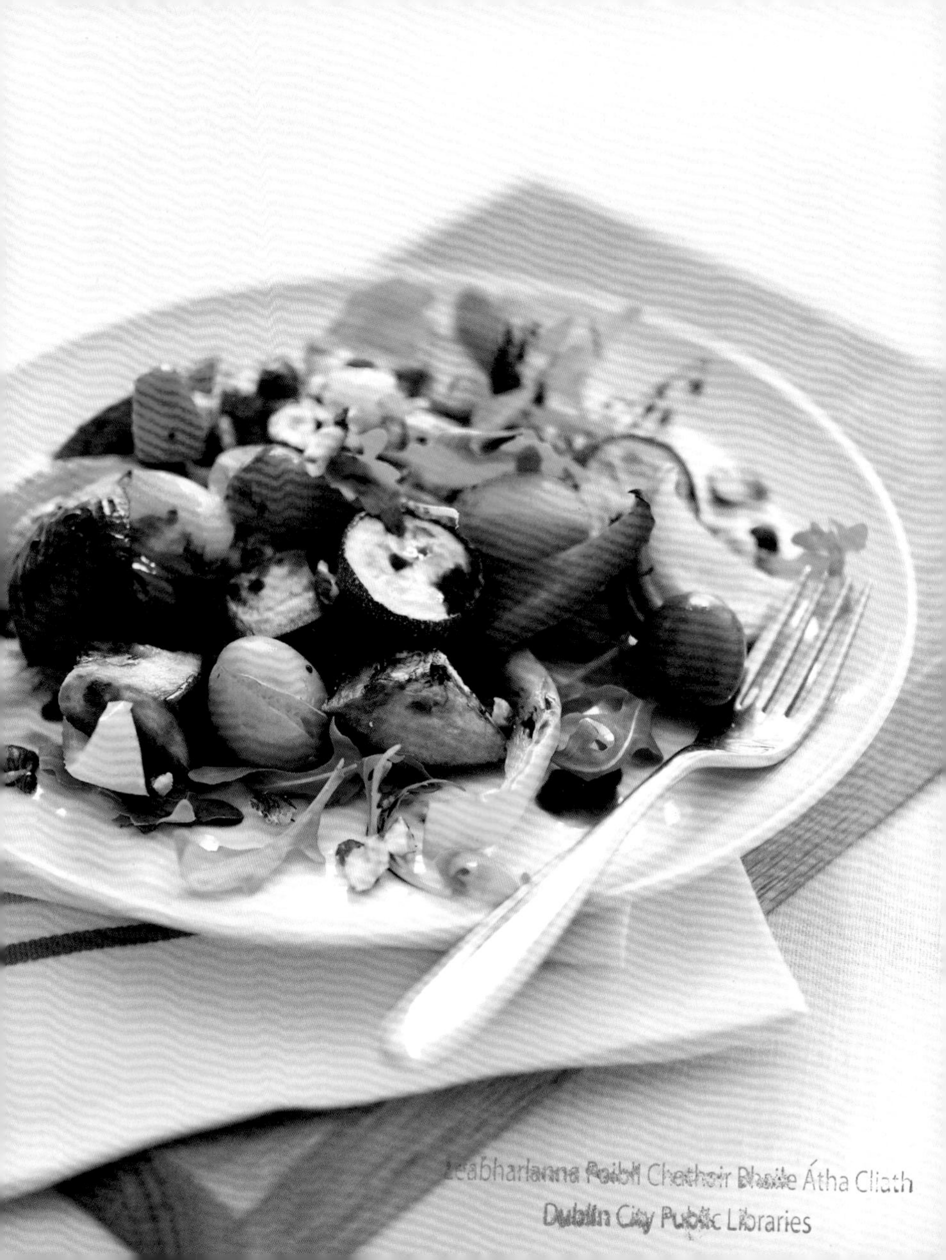

parsnip, sage & chestnut soup

Calories per serving **371**
Serves **4**
Preparation time **15 minutes**
Cooking time **50 minutes**

3 tablespoons ready-made
  or homemade **chilli oil**
  (see below for homemade),
  plus extra for drizzling
40 **sage leaves**
1 **leek**, trimmed, cleaned
  and chopped
500 g (1 lb) **parsnips**, roughly
  chopped
1.2 litres (2 pints) **vegetable
  stock**
pinch of ground **cloves**
200 g (7 oz) pack cooked
  peeled **chestnuts**
2 tablespoons **lemon juice**
crème fraîche, for topping
salt and **pepper**

Heat the chilli oil in a large saucepan until a sage leaf sizzles and crisps in 15–20 seconds and fry the remaining leaves in batches until crisp, lifting out with a slotted spoon onto a plate lined with kitchen paper. Set aside.

Add the leek and parsnips to the pan and fry gently for 10 minutes until softened. Add the stock and cloves and bring to the boil. Reduce the heat, cover and cook very gently for 30 minutes until the vegetables are very soft. Stir in the chestnuts and cook for a further 5 minutes.

Blend the soup using a stick blender or in a food processor. Add the lemon juice and reheat gently, seasoning to taste with salt and pepper.

Ladle into warmed bowls, top with a little crème fraîche and drizzle sparingly with extra chilli oil. Serve scattered with the sage leaves.

For homemade chilli oil, pour 300 ml (½ pint) olive oil into a saucepan. Add 6 whole dried chillies, 2 bay leaves and 1 rosemary sprig and heat through gently for 3 minutes. Remove from the heat and leave to cool completely. Using a jug or funnel, pour into a thoroughly clean glass jar with a clip top or cork seal, adding the chillies and herbs. Cover and store in a cool place for one week before using. The oil will become hotter during storage. Use as above, or in pasta and pizza recipes or any dishes where you want to add a little heat. **Calories per tablespoon 117**

quick one-pot ratatouille

Calories per serving **301**
Serves **4**
Preparation time **10 minutes**
Cooking time **20 minutes**

100 ml (3½ fl oz) **olive oil**
2 **onions**, chopped
1 **aubergine**, cut into
  bite-sized cubes
2 large **courgettes**, cut into
  bite-sized pieces
1 **red pepper**, cored,
  deseeded and cut into
  bite-sized pieces
1 **yellow pepper**, cored,
  deseeded and cut into
  bite-sized pieces
2 **garlic cloves**, crushed
400 g (13 oz) can **chopped
  tomatoes**
4 tablespoons chopped
  parsley or **basil**
salt and **pepper**

Heat the oil in a large saucepan until very hot. Add the onions, aubergine, courgettes, red and yellow peppers and garlic, and cook, stirring constantly, for a few minutes until softened. Add the tomatoes, season with salt and pepper and stir well.

Reduce the heat, cover the pan tightly and simmer for 15 minutes until all the vegetables are cooked. Remove from the heat and stir in the chopped parsley or basil before serving.

roasted stuffed peppers

Calories per serving **398**
Serves **2**
Preparation time **10 minutes**
Cooking time **55–60 minutes**

4 large **red peppers**
2 **garlic cloves**, crushed
1 tablespoon chopped **thyme**,
   plus extra to garnish
4 **plum tomatoes**, halved
4 tablespoons **extra-virgin
   olive oil**
2 tablespoons **balsamic
   vinegar**
salt and **pepper**

Cut the red peppers in half lengthways, then scoop out and discard the cores and seeds. Put the pepper halves, cut-sides up, in a roasting tin lined with foil or a ceramic dish. Divide the garlic and thyme between them and season with salt and pepper.

Put a tomato half in each pepper and drizzle with the oil and vinegar. Roast in a preheated oven, 220°C (425°F), Gas Mark 7, for 55–60 minutes until the peppers are soft and charred.

For cheesy roasted peppers, use a mixture of green, yellow and red peppers. After 45 minutes' cooking time, top each pepper with a slice of mozzarella cheese (about 60 g/2 oz in total) and return to the oven for the remaining 10–15 minutes. Serve with wedges of wholemeal soda bread. **Calories per serving 458**

thai squash, tofu & pea curry

Calories per serving **308**
Serves **4**
Preparation time **15 minutes**
Cooking time **25 minutes**

1 tablespoon **groundnut oil**
1 tablespoon **Thai red curry
  paste**
500 g (1 lb) peeled and
  deseeded **butternut
  squash**, cubed
450 ml (¾ pint) **vegetable
  stock**
400 ml (14 fl oz) **reduced-fat
  coconut milk**
6 **kaffir lime leaves**, bruised,
  plus extra shredded leaves
  to garnish
200 g (7 oz) fresh or frozen
  peas
300 g (10 oz) **firm tofu**, diced
2 tablespoons **light soy sauce**
juice of 1 **lime**

To garnish
coriander leaves
fresh **red chilli**, finely chopped

Heat the oil in a wok or deep frying pan, add the curry
paste and stir-fry over a low heat for 1 minute. Add the
butternut squash, stir-fry briefly and then add the stock,
coconut milk and lime leaves.

Bring to the boil, then cover, reduce the heat and
simmer gently for 15 minutes until the squash is tender.

Stir in the peas, tofu, soy sauce and lime juice and
simmer for a further 5 minutes until the peas are
cooked. Spoon into serving bowls and garnish with
shredded lime leaves, chopped coriander and red chilli.

For Thai green vegetable curry, use green curry
paste instead of red curry paste. Replace the butternut
squash with 1 sliced carrot, 1 sliced courgette and
1 cored, deseeded and sliced red pepper and follow
the recipe above. **Calories per serving 298**

greek vegetable casserole

Calories per serving **310**
  (not including bread)
Serves **4**
Preparation time **10 minutes**
Cooking time **25 minutes**

4 tablespoons **olive oil**
1 **onion**, thinly sliced
3 **peppers** of mixed colours,
  cored, deseeded and sliced
  into rings
4 **garlic cloves**, crushed
4 **tomatoes**, chopped
200 g (7 oz) **feta cheese**,
  cubed
1 teaspoon **dried oregano**
salt and **pepper**
chopped **flat-leaf parsley**,
  to garnish

Heat 3 tablespoons of the oil in a flameproof casserole, add the onion, peppers and garlic and cook until soft and starting to brown.

Add the tomatoes and cook for a few minutes until softened. Mix in the feta and oregano, season to taste with salt and pepper and drizzle with the remaining oil.

Cover and cook in a preheated oven, 200°C (400°F), Gas Mark 6, for 15 minutes. Garnish with the parsley and serve with warmed crusty bread, if liked.

For Middle Eastern vegetable casserole, heat 1 tablespoon olive oil in a flameproof casserole, add 1 red onion, cut into wedges, 3 sliced celery sticks and 3 thinly sliced carrots and cook until soft and starting to brown. Add 2 teaspoons harissa and cook, stirring, for 1 minute. Add about 625 g (1¼ lb) aubergines, trimmed and chopped, 2 large chopped tomatoes and 250 ml (8 fl oz) water. Bring to the boil, then cover and cook in a preheated oven, 180°C (350°F), Gas Mark 4, for about 25 minutes. Stir in 2 large potatoes, peeled and thickly sliced, and cook for a further 15 minutes or until tender but still firm. Serve hot, garnished with chopped coriander. **Calories per serving 246**

curried cauliflower with chickpeas

Calories per serving **310**
  (not including chapatis)
Serves **4**
Preparation time **10 minutes**
Cooking time **20 minutes**

2 tablespoons **olive oil**
1 **onion**, chopped
2 **garlic cloves**, crushed
4 tablespoons **medium curry
  paste**
1 small **cauliflower**, divided
  into florets
375 ml (13 fl oz) **vegetable
  stock**
4 **tomatoes**, roughly chopped
400 g (13 oz) canned
  chickpeas, rinsed and
  drained
2 tablespoons **mango
  chutney** (see right for
  homemade)
salt and **pepper**
4 tablespoons chopped
  coriander, to garnish

Heat the oil in a saucepan, add the onion and garlic and cook until the onion is soft and starting to brown. Stir in the curry paste, add the cauliflower and stock and bring to the boil. Reduce the heat, cover tightly and simmer for 10 minutes.

Add the tomatoes, chickpeas and chutney and continue to cook, uncovered, for 10 minutes. Season to taste with salt and pepper. Garnish with coriander and serve with rolled chapatis, if liked.

For homemade mango chutney, put the peeled, stoned and sliced flesh of 6 ripe mangoes in a large saucepan with 300 ml (½ pint) white wine vinegar and cook over a low heat for 10 minutes. Add 250 g (8 oz) soft dark brown sugar, 50 g (2 oz) fresh root ginger, peeled and finely chopped, 2 crushed garlic cloves, 2 teaspoons chilli powder and 1 teaspoon salt and bring to the boil, stirring constantly. Reduce the heat and simmer for 30 minutes, stirring occasionally. Ladle into a sterilized screw-top jar and replace the lid. Store in the refrigerator and use within 1 month. **Calories for whole jar 449**

pumpkin with walnut pesto

Calories per serving **318**
Serves **4**
Preparation time **15 minutes**
Cooking time **20–25 minutes**

1 kg (2 lb) **pumpkin**
extra-virgin olive oil, for
  brushing
salt and **pepper**

Walnut pesto
50 g (2 oz) **walnuts**, toasted
2 **spring onions**, trimmed
  and chopped
1 large **garlic clove**, crushed
50 g (2 oz) **rocket leaves**,
  plus extra to serve
3 tablespoons **walnut oil**
3 tablespoons **extra-virgin
  olive oil**

Cut the pumpkin into 8 wedges. Remove the seeds and fibre but leave the skin on. Brush all over with olive oil, season with salt and pepper and spread out on a large baking sheet. Roast in a preheated oven, 220°C (425°F), Gas Mark 7, for 20–25 minutes until tender, turning halfway through.

Meanwhile, make the pesto. Put the walnuts, spring onions, garlic and rocket in a food processor and process until finely chopped. With the motor running, gradually drizzle in the oils. Season the pesto with salt and pepper.

Serve the roasted pumpkin with the pesto and extra rocket leaves.

For gnocchi with walnut pesto as a starter, make
the pesto as in the recipe above. Prepare and cook 400 g (13 oz) fresh store-bought gnocchi according to the package instructions or until the gnocchi rise to the surface, then drain, transfer to a buttered serving dish and top with the pesto. **Calories per serving 439**

cream of leek & pea soup

Calories per serving **322**
Serves **4**
Preparation time **15 minutes**
Cooking time **20 minutes**

2 tablespoons **olive oil**
375 g (12 oz) **leeks**, slit, well
  washed and thinly sliced
375 g (12 oz) fresh shelled
  or frozen **peas**
900 ml (1 ½ pints) **vegetable
  stock**
small bunch of **mint**
150 g (5 oz) **full-fat
  mascarpone cheese**
grated rind of 1 small **lemon**
salt and **pepper**

To garnish (optional)
mint leaves
lemon rind curls

Heat the oil in a saucepan, add the leeks, toss in the oil then cover and fry gently for 10 minutes, stirring occasionally, until softened but not coloured. Mix in the peas and cook briefly.

Pour the stock into the pan, add a little salt and pepper then bring to the boil. Cover and simmer gently for 10 minutes. Ladle half the soup into a blender or food processor, add all the mint and blend until smooth. Pour the purée back into the saucepan.

Mix the mascarpone with half the lemon rind, reserving the rest for a garnish. Spoon half the mixture into the soup, then reheat, stirring until the mascarpone has melted. Taste and adjust the seasoning if needed. Ladle the soup into warmed bowls, top with spoonfuls of the remaining mascarpone and a sprinkling of the remaining lemon rind. Garnish with mint leaves and lemon rind curls, if liked.

For cream of leek, pea & watercress soup, use 175 g (6 oz) peas and add a roughly chopped bunch of watercress. Simmer in 600 ml (1 pint) of vegetable stock then, instead of adding the mascarpone, stir in 150 ml (¼ pint) milk and 150 ml (¼ pint) double cream, drizzling a little extra cream over at the end.
Calories per serving 327

baked aubergines with tzatziki

Calories per serving **325**
Serves **4**
Preparation time **10 minutes,
  plus cooling**
Cooking time **50 minutes**

2 large **aubergines**, halved
  lengthways
1 tablespoon **olive oil**
100 g (3½ oz) **couscous**
175 ml (6 fl oz) **boiling water**
1 **onion**, finely chopped
1 **garlic clove**, crushed
100 g (3½ oz) **ready-to-eat
  dried apricots**, chopped
50 g (2 oz) **raisins**
grated rind and juice of
  1 **lemon**
2 tablespoons chopped **mint**
2 tablespoons chopped
  coriander
2 tablespoons freshly grated
  Parmesan cheese
4 **flat breads**, to serve

Tzatziki
½ **cucumber**, finely chopped
2 **spring onions**, sliced
200 ml (7 fl oz) **Greek yogurt**

Place the aubergines cut-side up on a baking sheet and brush each with a little of the oil. Cook in a preheated oven, 200°C (400°F), Gas Mark 6, for 30–35 minutes until the flesh is tender, then remove (leaving the oven on) and leave to cool. When the aubergines are cool enough to handle, scoop out the flesh and roughly chop. Reserve the skins.

Place the couscous in a heatproof container, meanwhile. pour on the measurement water and cover with clingfilm. Set aside for 5 minutes, then remove the clingfilm and fork through.

Heat the remaining oil in a nonstick frying pan, add the onion and garlic and fry for 3 minutes, then stir through the apricots, raisins, lemon rind and juice, couscous, herbs, Parmesan and aubergine flesh.

Spoon this mixture into the aubergine skins and return them to the oven for 10 minutes.

Mix together the tzatziki ingredients in a serving bowl and serve with the aubergines and flat breads.

For a spiced tomato sauce to serve with the aubergines instead of the tzatziki, heat 2 teaspoons olive oil in a saucepan and use to cook 1 sliced onion for 5 minutes until beginning to soften. Add ½ teaspoon each of ground cinnamon, ground cumin and ground ginger and cook for a further minute. Stir in a 400 g (13 oz) can chopped tomatoes and bring to the boil. Simmer, uncovered, for 20 minutes, then remove from the heat and season to taste with salt and harissa paste. Serve warm or at room temperature. **Calories per serving 53**

charred leek salad with hazelnuts

Calories per serving **341**
Serves **4**
Preparation time **10 minutes**
Cooking time **12–16 minutes**

500 g (1 lb) **baby leeks**
1–2 tablespoons **hazelnut oil**
dash of **lemon juice**
40 g (1 ½ oz) blanched
   hazelnuts
2 **Little Gem** or **cos lettuce
hearts**
a few **mint sprigs**
15 g (½ oz) **pecorino cheese**
20 **black olives**, to garnish

Dressing
4 tablespoons **hazelnut oil**
2 tablespoons **extra-virgin
olive oil**
2 teaspoons **sherry vinegar**
salt and **pepper**

Brush the leeks with the hazelnut oil. Cook, in batches, on a preheated hot ridged griddle pan or under a preheated hot grill, turning frequently, for 6–8 minutes until evenly browned and cooked through. Toss with the lemon juice and season with salt and pepper. Leave to cool.

Heat a heavy-based frying pan until hot meanwhile, add the hazelnuts and cook over a medium heat, stirring, for 3–4 minutes until browned. Leave to cool slightly and then roughly chop. Separate the lettuce leaves and pull the mint leaves from the sprigs.

Arrange the leeks in serving bowls or on plates and top with the lettuce leaves, mint and hazelnuts. Whisk all the dressing ingredients together in a small bowl, season with salt and pepper and pour over the salad. Shave the pecorino over the salad and serve garnished with the olives.

For charred asparagus salad with pine nuts,
replace the leeks with the same quantity of trimmed asparagus. Brush with extra-virgin olive oil rather than hazelnut oil, and cook and dress as in the recipe above. Toast pine nuts instead of hazelnuts, and use tarragon leaves in place of mint. For the dressing, use 4 tablespoons extra-virgin olive oil, 2 tablespoons grapeseed oil, 2 teaspoons tarragon vinegar and the grated rind of 1 lemon, reserving a few thin strips of rind. Shave a little Parmesan cheese over the salad and garnish with the reserved lemon rind strips.
Calories per serving 350

walnut & blue cheese salad

Calories per serving **343**
Serves **4**
Preparation time **15 minutes**
Cooking time **5 minutes**

50 g (2 oz) **walnut halves**
2 tablespoons **icing sugar**
2 **chicory heads**
50 g (2 oz) **rocket leaves**
1 **radicchio**, separated into
   leaves
125 g (4 oz) **blue cheese**,
   such as **Roquefort**

Dressing
1 teaspoon **Dijon mustard**
2 tablespoons **cider vinegar**
4 tablespoons **olive oil**

Put the walnuts in a plastic food bag with the icing sugar and 1 tablespoon water and shake them until coated. Arrange the nuts on a baking sheet and roast in a preheated oven, 180°C (350°F), Gas Mark 4, for 5 minutes or until gold and crusted.

Separate the chicory leaves and put them into a large salad bowl with the rocket and radicchio. Crumble over the cheese and add the walnuts. Toss carefully.

Make the dressing by whisking together the mustard, vinegar and oil. Drizzle the dressing over the salad, mix lightly and serve.

For griddled radicchio & chicory salad, cut 2 chicory heads in half and 2 radicchio into quarters. Dust well with 2 tablespoons icing sugar and place on an oiled griddle over a medium heat. Griddle the chicory heads and radicchio until golden and caramelized. Combine 3 tablespoons cider vinegar and 4 tablespoons olive oil with 20 g (¾ oz) sultanas and heat them in a small saucepan. Pour over the salad and combine well. Garnish with 3 tablespoons roughly chopped parsley and 125 g (4 oz) crumbled Gorgonzola cheese. **Calories per serving 273**

lentil moussaka

Calories per serving **304**
Serves **4**
Preparation time **10 minutes**
Cooking time **45 minutes,**
  plus standing

125 g (4 oz) **dried brown**
  or **green lentils**, rinsed
  and drained
400 g (13 oz) can **chopped**
  tomatoes
2 **garlic cloves**, crushed
½ teaspoon **dried oregano**
pinch of **ground nutmeg**
150 ml (¼ pint) **vegetable**
  stock
2–3 tablespoons **vegetable oil**
250 g (8 oz) **aubergine**, sliced
1 **onion**, finely chopped

Cheese topping
1 **egg**
150 g (5 oz) **soft cheese**
pinch of **ground nutmeg**
salt and **pepper**

Put the lentils in a saucepan with the tomatoes, garlic, oregano and nutmeg. Pour in the stock. Bring to the boil, then reduce the heat and simmer for 20 minutes until the lentils are tender but not mushy, topping up with extra stock as needed.

Meanwhile, heat the oil in a frying pan and lightly fry the aubergine and onion, until the onion is soft and the aubergine is golden on both sides.

Layer the aubergine mixture and lentil mixture alternately in an ovenproof dish.

Make the topping. In a bowl, beat together the egg, cheese and nutmeg with a good dash of salt and pepper. Pour over the moussaka and cook in a preheated oven, 200°C (400°F), Gas Mark 6, for 20–25 minutes. Remove from the oven and leave to stand for 5 minutes before serving with salad leaves.

For moussaka jacket potatoes, cook 4 scrubbed baking potatoes, about 200 g (7 oz) in total, in a preheated oven, 200°C (400°F), Gas Mark 6, for about 1 hour until tender, or microwave if preferred. Meanwhile, make the lentil mixture as above. Fry the aubergine and onion separately, then stir into the lentils when cooked. Spoon over the slit potatoes, then top each one with a spoonful of soft cheese and a sprinkling of grated Cheddar cheese. **Calories per serving 481**

sweetcorn & pepper frittata

Calories per serving **347**
  **(not including salad
  and bread)**
Serves **4**
Preparation time **10 minutes**
Cooking time **about
10 minutes**

2 tablespoons **olive oil**
4 **spring onions**, thinly sliced
200 g (7 oz) can **sweetcorn**,
  drained
150 g (5 oz) bottled **roasted
  red peppers** in oil, drained
  and cut into strips
4 **eggs**, lightly beaten
125 g (4 oz) **strong Cheddar
  cheese**, grated
small handful of **chives**,
  finely chopped
salt and **pepper**

Heat the oil in a frying pan, add the spring onions,
sweetcorn and red peppers and cook for 30 seconds.

Add the eggs, Cheddar, chives, and salt and pepper
to taste and cook over a medium heat for 4–5 minutes
until the base is set. Remove from the hob, place under
a preheated grill and cook for 3–4 minutes or until
golden and set. Cut into wedges and serve immediately
with a green salad and crusty bread, if liked.

For courgette, pepper & Gruyère frittata, use
200 g (7 oz) finely chopped courgettes instead of the
sweetcorn, 125 g (4 oz) grated Gruyère cheese in place
of the Cheddar and substitute 4 tablespoons chopped
mint leaves for the chives. **Calories per serving 305**

mushrooms à la grecque

Calories per serving **347**
Serves **4**
Preparation time **10 minutes,**
   plus standing
Cooking time **10 minutes**

8 tablespoons **olive oil**
2 large **onions**, sliced
3 **garlic cloves**, finely chopped
600 g (1 lb 3½ oz) **button**
   mushrooms, halved
8 **plum tomatoes,** roughly
   chopped or 400 g (13 oz)
   can **chopped tomatoes**
100 g (3½ oz) **pitted black**
   olives
2 tablespoons **white wine**
   vinegar
salt and **pepper**
chopped **parsley**, to garnish

Heat 2 tablespoons of the oil in a large frying pan, add
the onions and garlic and cook until soft and starting
to brown. Add the mushrooms and tomatoes and cook,
stirring gently, for 4–5 minutes. Remove from the heat.

Transfer the mushroom mixture to a serving dish and
garnish with the olives.

Whisk the remaining oil with the vinegar in a small bowl,
season to taste with salt and pepper and drizzle over the
salad. Garnish with the chopped parsley, cover and leave
to stand at room temperature for 30 minutes to allow
the flavours to mingle before serving.

For mushroom pasta salad, prepare the mushroom
mixture as above. Cook 200 g (7 oz) dried pennette
or farfalle in a large saucepan of salted boiling water
according to the packet instructions until al dente.
Meanwhile, cook 125 g (4 oz) green beans in a saucepan
of salted boiling water until just tender. Drain the beans,
refresh under cold running water, and drain again. Drain
the pasta thoroughly and toss into the mushroom mixture
with the beans and 2 tablespoons torn basil leaves. Serve
at room temperature. **Calories per serving 357**

fig, bean & toasted pecan salad

Calories per serving **352**
Serves **4**
Preparation time **5 minutes,
plus cooling**
Cooking time **5–6 minutes**

100 g (3½ oz) **pecan nuts**
200 g (7 oz) **green beans**,
trimmed
4 **fresh figs**, cut into quarters
100 g (3½ oz) **rocket leaves**
small handful of **mint leaves**
50 g (2 oz) **Parmesan** or
pecorino cheese

Dressing
3 tablespoons **walnut oil**
2 teaspoons **sherry vinegar**
1 teaspoon **vincotto**
salt and **pepper**

Heat a heavy-based frying pan over a medium heat, add the pecan nuts and dry-fry, stirring frequently, for 3–4 minutes or until browned. Tip onto a small plate and leave to cool.

Cook the beans in a saucepan of lightly salted boiling water for 2 minutes. Drain, refresh under cold running water and pat dry with kitchen paper. Put the beans in a bowl with the figs, pecan nuts, rocket and mint.

Whisk together all the dressing ingredients in a small bowl and season with salt and paper. If you can't find vincotto, use balsamic vinegar as an alternative. Pour over the salad and toss well. Shave over the Parmesan or pecorino and serve.

For mixed bean salad, combine 200 g (7 oz) cooked trimmed green beans with 2 x 400 g (13 oz) cans drained mixed beans, 4 finely chopped spring onions, 1 crushed garlic clove and 4 tablespoons chopped mixed herbs, then dress with 4 tablespoons olive oil, the juice of ½ lemon, a pinch of caster sugar and salt and pepper to taste. **Calories per serving 259**

chickpea & pepper salad

Calories per serving **360**
   (not including tzatziki)
Serves **4**
Preparation time **25 minutes**
Cooking time **35 minutes**

2 x 400 g (13 oz) cans
   chickpeas
2 **red peppers**
1 **yellow pepper**
1 **red onion**
4 **plum tomatoes**, cut into
   wedges
olive oil
2 tablespoons **fennel seeds**
small bunch of **parsley**,
   chopped
salt and **pepper**
tzatziki (see below), to serve
   (optional)

Dressing
4 tablespoons **sherry vinegar**
3 tablespoons **olive oil**
1 **garlic clove**, crushed
½ teaspoon **ground cumin**

Rinse the chickpeas in cold water and leave to drain. Core and deseed the peppers and cut the flesh into 2 cm (¾ inch) strips. Cut the onion in half and then cut each half into quarters, leaving the root on so that the wedges stay together.

Drizzle the peppers, onion and tomatoes with olive oil and season with salt and pepper. Heat a griddle pan over a high heat and cook the peppers for 2 minutes on each side. Place the peppers in an ovenproof dish and cook the onion in the same way. Place the onion and tomatoes with the peppers, sprinkle with the fennel seeds and cook in a preheated oven, 180°C (350°F), Gas Mark 4, for 20 minutes until done.

Meanwhile, make the dressing. Whisk together the vinegar and oil with the crushed garlic and cumin. Transfer the drained chickpeas to a large salad bowl and mix in the hot vegetables and chopped parsley. Season to taste with salt and pepper, drizzle over the dressing and stir to combine. Serve with a dollop of tzatziki, if liked (see below).

For tzatziki to serve with the above salad, cut a cucumber in half lengthways and remove the seeds with a spoon. Finely dice the flesh and mix it with 250 ml (8 fl oz) Greek yogurt, 1 crushed garlic clove, 1 tablespoon olive oil, 2 tablespoons chopped mint and 1 tablespoon lemon juice. Season to taste with salt and pepper, cover and leave in the refrigerator for at least 1 hour before serving. **Calories per serving 94**

thai red tofu & vegetable curry

Calories per serving **364**
  (not including rice)
Serves **4**
Preparation time **15 minutes**
Cooking time **25–30 minutes**

450 g (14½ oz) **firm tofu**
1 tablespoon **rapeseed oil**
2 tablespoons ready-made
  Thai red curry paste
1–2 fresh **green chillies**,
  sliced
200 ml (7 fl oz) canned
  reduced-fat coconut milk
250 ml (8 fl oz) **vegetable
  stock**
1 large **aubergine**, diced
12 **baby sweetcorn**
100 g (3½ oz) **mangetout**
100 g (3½ oz) **carrots**, sliced
125 g (4 oz) **shiitake
  mushrooms**, halved
1 large **green pepper**, sliced
150 g (5 oz) canned sliced
  bamboo shoots, drained
1 tablespoon **Thai fish sauce**
1 tablespoon **clear honey**
2 **kaffir lime leaves**

To garnish
handful of **Thai basil leaves**
handful of **cashew nuts**,
  toasted

Drain the tofu and pat it dry with kitchen paper before cutting it into 5 cm (2 inch) cubes.

Heat the oil in a wok over high heat until the oil starts to shimmer. Stir-fry the red curry paste and chillies for 1 minute, then stir in 2 tablespoons of the coconut milk (from the thicker part at the top of the can) and cook, stirring constantly, for 2 minutes.

Add the stock and bring to the boil. Add the aubergine, then bring the mixture back to the boil and simmer for about 5 minutes. Add the remaining vegetables and cook for another 5–10 minutes. Stir in the fish sauce, honey, lime leaves and the remaining coconut milk and simmer for another 5 minutes, stirring occasionally. Add the tofu cubes and mix well.

Garnish with torn Thai basil leaves and toasted cashew nuts. Serve with jasmine or sticky (glutinous) rice, if liked, which will absorb the wonderful aromatic sauce.

For one-pot tofu & vegetable noodles, use 400 ml (14 fl oz) reduced-fat coconut milk and increase the quantity of stock to 350 ml (12 fl oz). Add 150 g (5 oz) cooked thick rice noodles along with the tofu and simmer for 1 minute before serving with the garnish above. **Calories per serving 499**

italian bean & artichoke salad

Calories per serving **367**
Serves **2**
Preparation time **10 minutes**

400 g (13 oz) can **artichoke hearts**
1 small **red onion**, sliced
100 g (3 oz) ball **mozzarella cheese**, cubed
400 g (13 oz) can **cannellini beans**, rinsed and drained
75 g (3 oz) **rocket leaves**

Dressing
1 fresh **red chilli**, finely chopped
1 teaspoon **cider vinegar**
1 teaspoon **Dijon mustard**
1 teaspoon **caster sugar**
1 tablespoon **olive oil**
1 tablespoon chopped fresh **mixed herbs** (such as **parsley, coriander** and **basil**)

Make the dressing. Whisk together the chilli, vinegar, mustard, sugar, oil and chopped herbs in a small bowl. Set aside.

Drain the artichoke hearts and mix them with the onion, mozzarella and beans. Add the rocket and combine.

Stir the dressing through the salad and serve.

For quick bean & feta salad, cut 2 thick slices of bread into cubes. Brush them with 1 tablespoon olive oil, transfer to a roasting tin and cook in a preheated oven, 200°C (400°F), Gas Mark 6, for 10–15 minutes until golden. Combine a 200 g (7 oz) can mixed bean salad with 50 g (2 oz) chopped feta cheese. Serve with chopped cos lettuce and a handful of croûtons.
Calories per serving 285

butter bean & tomato soup

Calories per serving **379**
  (not including bread)
Serves **4**
Preparation time **10 minutes**
Cooking time **20 minutes**

3 tablespoons **olive oil**
1 **onion**, finely chopped
2 **celery sticks**, thinly sliced
2 **garlic cloves**, thinly sliced
2 x 400 g (13 oz) cans **butter
  beans**, rinsed and drained
4 tablespoons **sun-dried
  tomato paste**
900 ml (1 ½ pints) **vegetable
  stock**
1 tablespoon chopped **thyme**
  or **rosemary,** plus extra
  leaves to garnish
salt and **pepper**
Parmesan cheese shavings,
  to serve

Heat the oil in a saucepan over a medium heat, add the onion and fry for 3 minutes or until softened. Add the celery and garlic and fry for 2 minutes.

Add the butter beans, sun-dried tomato paste, stock, rosemary or thyme and season with salt and pepper. Bring to the boil, then reduce the heat, cover and simmer gently for 15 minutes.

Ladle into warmed bowls and serve sprinkled with Parmesan shavings and extra thyme or rosemary leaves. This soup makes a light main course served with bread, if liked.

For spiced carrot & lentil soup, heat 2 tablespoons oil in a saucepan, add 1 chopped onion, 2 crushed garlic cloves and 375 g (12 oz) chopped carrots and fry for 10 minutes. Add a 400 g (13 oz) can lentils, drained, 2 teaspoons ground coriander, 1 teaspoon ground cumin and 1 tablespoon chopped thyme and fry for 1 minute. Stir in 1 litre (1¾ pints) vegetable stock, a 400 g (13 oz) can chopped tomatoes and 2 teaspoons lemon juice and bring to the boil. Cover and simmer gently for 20 minutes. Put in a blender or food processor and blend until smooth, then return to the pan and warm through. **Calories per serving 240**

lentil & feta salad

Calories per serving **386**
Serves **2–4**
Preparation time **15 minutes**
Cooking time **30 minutes**

250 g (8 oz) **Puy lentils**
2 **carrots**, finely diced
2 **celery sticks**, finely diced
100 g (3½ oz) **feta cheese**
2 tablespoons chopped
  parsley

Dressing
3 tablespoons **white wine**
  vinegar
2 teaspoons **Dijon mustard**
5 tablespoons **olive oil**
salt and **pepper**

Put the lentils in a saucepan, cover with cold water
and add a pinch of salt. Bring to the boil and cook for
20–25 minutes until just cooked but not mushy. Drain
and refresh in cold water, then drain again and transfer
to a large salad bowl.

Add the carrots and celery to the bowl with the lentils.
Crumble in the feta and add the chopped parsley.

Make the dressing by whisking the vinegar, mustard
and oil. Add the dressing to the salad and stir to
combine well. Season to taste with salt and pepper
and serve immediately.

For lentil salad with poached egg & asparagus,
prepare the lentils as above. Blanch about 500 g
(1 lb) asparagus, woody ends removed, then refresh
and reserve. Slice the asparagus into 3 cm (1¼ inch)
pieces, add it to the lentils with 2 tablespoons chopped
parsley and 5 tablespoons olive oil and season with salt
and pepper. Toss carefully to combine and transfer to
serving plates. Put a poached egg on each salad and
serve with 1 tablespoon of hollandaise sauce on top
of the egg. **Calories per serving 492**

chickpea & herb salad

Calories per serving **389**
Serves **4**
Preparation time **10 minutes**,
   plus cooling
Cooking time **10 minutes**

100 g (3½ oz) **bulgar wheat**
4 tablespoons **olive oil**
1 tablespoon **lemon juice**
2 tablespoons chopped
   flat-leaf parsley
1 tablespoon chopped **mint**
400 g (13 oz) can **chickpeas**,
   rinsed and drained
125 g (4 oz) **cherry tomatoes**,
   halved
1 tablespoon chopped **mild**
   onion
100 g (3½ oz) **cucumber**
150 g (5 oz) **feta cheese**,
   diced
salt and **pepper**

Put the bulgar wheat in a heatproof bowl and pour over sufficient boiling water just to cover. Set aside until the water has been absorbed. If you want to give a fluffier finish to the bulgar wheat, transfer it to a steamer and steam for 5 minutes. Spread on a plate to cool.

Mix together the olive oil, lemon juice, parsley and mint in a large salad bowl. Season to taste with salt and pepper. Add the the chickpeas, tomatoes, onion and bulgar wheat.

Dice the cucumber and add to the bowl. Mix well and add the feta, stirring lightly to avoid breaking up the cheese. Serve immediately.

For beetroot & chickpea salad, combine 150 g (5 oz) baby chard with a 400 g (13 oz) can rinsed and drained chickpeas, 200 g (7 oz) precooked and diced beetroots in a large mixing bowl. Cut an orange in half and put the halves on a hot griddle pan until golden but not black. Squeeze the juice into a small bowl and add 1 teaspoon clear honey and 3 tablespoons olive oil. Whisk together, then dress the salad lightly and crumble over 150 g (5 oz) feta.
Calories per serving 304

greek country salad with haloumi

Calories per serving **398**
Serves **4**
Preparation time **10 minutes**
Cooking time **2 minutes**

4 **vine-ripened tomatoes**,
 roughly chopped
½ **onion**, sliced
1 **Lebanese cucumber**,
 thickly sliced
100 g (3½ oz) pitted **black
 Kalamata olives**
1 small **cos lettuce**
250 g (8 oz) **haloumi cheese**,
 sliced

Dressing
4 tablespoons **extra-virgin
 olive oil**
1½ tablespoons **red wine
 vinegar**
1 teaspoon **dried oregano**
salt and **pepper**

Put the tomatoes, onion, cucumber and olives in a bowl. Tear the lettuce into pieces and add to the salad. Toss well and arrange on a large platter.

Whisk all the dressing ingredients together in a small bowl and season with salt and pepper. Drizzle a little over the salad.

Heat a heavy-based frying pan until hot, add the haloumi slices and cook for 1 minute on each side until they are charred and softened. Arrange on top of the salad, drizzle over the remaining dressing and serve immediately.

For Greek salad with chunky croûtons, replace the haloumi with 200 g (7 oz) crumbled feta cheese. To make the croûtons, cut thick slices of close-textured country bread, then cut these into large chunks. Heat a little olive oil in a frying pan and fry the bread, turning occasionally, until crisp and golden. Add extra olive oil as needed. Cool, then toss into the salad and serve immediately. **Calories per serving 410**

pepper & aubergine hummus

Calories per serving **343**
  (not including bread)
Serves **4**
Preparation time **10 minutes,**
  plus cooling
Cooking time **45–50 minutes**

1 **red pepper**, cored,
  deseeded and quartered
3 **garlic cloves**, unpeeled and
  lightly crushed
1 **aubergine**, cut into large
  chunks
1 tablespoon **chilli oil**, plus
  extra to serve
½ tablespoon **fennel seeds**
  (optional)
400 g (13 oz) can **chickpeas,**
  rinsed and drained
1 tablespoon **tahini**
1 teaspoon **sesame seeds**,
  lightly toasted
salt and **pepper**

To serve
4 **wholemeal pitta breads**
olive oil spray
1 teaspoon **paprika**

Put the pepper, garlic and aubergine in a single layer in a large roasting tin. Drizzle with the chilli oil and sprinkle with the fennel seeds, if using, and season with salt and pepper. Place in a preheated oven, 190°C (375°F), Gas Mark 5, for 35–40 minutes or until softened and golden. Remove from the oven but do not turn it off.

Peel the skins from the garlic cloves and put in a blender or food processor with the roasted vegetables, three-quarters of the chickpeas and the tahini. Blend until almost smooth, season to taste and then spoon into a serving bowl. Cover with clingfilm and leave to cool.

Cut the pitta bread into 2.5 cm (1 inch) strips and place in a large bowl. Spray with a little olive oil and toss with the paprika and a little salt until well coated. Arrange in a single layer on a baking sheet. Toast in the oven for 10–12 minutes or until crisp.

Sprinkle the hummus with the remaining chickpeas and the sesame seeds and drizzle with 1–2 tablespoons chilli oil. Serve with the toasted pitta breads, if liked.

For roasted artichoke & pepper hummus, replace the aubergine with a drained 400 g (13 oz) can artichoke hearts in water. Roast in the oven with the peppers and garlic, as above, replacing the chilli oil with 1 tablespoon lemon-infused oil. Omit the fennel seeds. Continue as above. **Calories per serving 356**

garlic & caramelized onion bhajis

Calories per bhaji **310**
Makes **6**
Preparation time **20 minutes**
Cooking time **5 minutes**

2 tablespoons **olive oil**
1 **onion**, sliced
2 **garlic cloves**, sliced
1 teaspoon **cumin seeds**
2 tablespoons chopped
  coriander
200 g (7 oz) **chickpea/
  gram flour**
1 teaspoon **bicarbonate
  of soda**
½ teaspoon **salt**

Heat half the oil in a nonstick frying pan, add the onion, garlic and cumin seeds and fry for 5–6 minutes until golden and softened. Stir through the coriander.

Meanwhile, mix together the flour, bicarbonate of soda, salt and 250 ml (8 fl oz) water in a bowl and set aside for 10 minutes, then stir it into the onion mixture.

Heat a little of the remaining oil in the frying pan and add spoonfuls of the mix, frying for 2–3 minutes, turning halfway through cooking. Cook the remaining mix in the same way.

For a herb & yogurt chutney to serve with the bhajis, blend 2 tablespoons yogurt, a handful of mint leaves and a handful of coriander leaves in a blender or food processor with 1 tablespoon lemon juice, until smooth. Stir into a bowl with another 4 tablespoons natural yogurt and season with salt. Cover and keep chilled until ready to serve the bhajis. **Calories per serving 24**

split pea & pepper patties

Calories per serving **312**
Serves **4**
Preparation time **15 minutes,
plus chilling**
Cooking time **45–50 minutes**

750 ml (1 ¼ pints) **vegetable
stock**
3 **garlic cloves**
250 g (8 oz) **yellow split peas**
olive oil spray
2 **red peppers**, halved, cored
and deseeded
1 **yellow pepper**, halved,
cored and deseeded
1 **red onion**, quartered
1 tablespoon chopped **mint**,
plus extra leaves to garnish
2 tablespoons **capers**, drained
and chopped
flour, for dusting
salt and **pepper**

Tzatziki
½ **cucumber**, finely chopped
1 **garlic clove**, crushed
2 tablespoons chopped **mint**
300 ml (½ pint) **low-fat
natural yogurt**

Bring the stock to the boil in a large saucepan. Peel and halve 1 of the garlic cloves, then add to the pan with the split peas and cook for 40 minutes until the split peas are tender. Season with salt and pepper and leave to cool slightly.

Meanwhile, lightly spray a roasting tin with oil. Place the remaining garlic cloves in the tin with the peppers and onion and cook in a preheated oven, 200°C (400°F), Gas Mark 6, for 20 minutes. Squeeze the roasted garlic cloves from their skins and chop with the roasted vegetables.

Mix together the split peas, roasted vegetables, mint and capers in a large bowl. Flour your hands and shape the mixture into 12 patties. Chill until ready to cook.

For the tzatziki, mix the ingredients together, cover and chill in the refrigerator for 30 minutes before serving.

Heat a frying pan and spray with oil. Cook the patties, in batches if necessary, for 2 minutes on each side. Serve 3 patties per person, hot or cold, garnished with mint leaves and with a small bowl of tzatziki.

sweet potatoes & tomato salsa

Calories per serving **384**
Serves **2**
Preparation time **5 minutes**
Cooking time **45 minutes**

2 large **sweet potatoes**,
  each about 275 g (9 oz)
50 g (2 oz) **Emmental** or
  Cheddar cheese, grated
salt

Tomato salsa
2 large **tomatoes**, finely
  chopped
½ small **red onion**, finely
  chopped
1 **celery stick**, finely chopped
small handful of **coriander**,
  chopped
2 tablespoons **lime juice**
2 teaspoons **caster sugar**

Scrub the potatoes and put them in a small roasting tin. Prick with a fork and sprinkle with a little salt. Bake in a preheated oven, 200°C (400°F), Gas Mark 6, for 45 minutes until tender. (If you do not have the time to bake the sweet potatoes, they can be microwaved like ordinary ones, although this way you will lose the wonderful crispy baked flavour. Prick them with a fork and cook on the highest setting for 15–20 minutes, or according to the microwave manufacturer's instructions.)

Meanwhile, make the salsa. Mix the tomatoes in a bowl with the onion, celery, coriander, lime juice and sugar.

Halve the potatoes and fluff up the flesh with a fork. Sprinkle with the cheese and top with the salsa.

For sweet potatoes with coriander dressing, bake the potatoes as above. Omit the tomato salsa and cheese. Make a dressing by combining 100 g (3½ oz) half-fat crème fraîche, 4 sliced spring onions, a handful of chopped coriander, and the rind and juice of 1 lime. Plate and fluff up the halved potatoes and serve with a generous dollop of dressing. **Calories per serving 342**

recipes under 500 calories

baked sweet potatoes

Calories per serving **405**
Serves **4**
Preparation time **5 minutes**
Cooking time **45–50 minutes**

4 **sweet potatoes**, about
   250 g (8 oz) each, scrubbed
200 g (7 oz) **soured cream**
2 **spring onions**, trimmed and
   finely chopped
1 tablespoon chopped **chives**
50 g (2 oz) **butter**
salt and **pepper**

Put the potatoes in a roasting tin and roast in a preheated oven, 220°C (425°F), Gas Mark 7, for 45–50 minutes until cooked through.

Combine the soured cream, spring onions, chives and salt and pepper in a bowl.

Cut the baked potatoes in half lengthways, top with the butter and spoon over the soured cream mixture. Serve immediately.

For crispy sweet potato skins, allow the baked sweet potatoes to cool, cut into wedges and scoop out some of the soft potato (and use elsewhere), leaving a good lining inside the skin. Deep fry in hot oil for 4–5 minutes until crisp. Serve with soured cream and chopped chives to dip. **Calories per serving 444**

grilled vegetable & haloumi salad

Calories per serving **416**
Serves **4**
Preparation time **15 minutes**
Cooking time **25 minutes**

12 **cherry tomatoes** on
  the vine
4 **portobello mushrooms**
olive oil
2 **courgettes**, cut into
  batons about 4 x 2 cm
  (1½ x ¾ inches)
500 g (1 lb) fresh **asparagus**,
  trimmed
250 g (8 oz) **haloumi cheese**,
  cut into 5 mm (¼ inch) slices
salt and **pepper**

Dressing
2 tablespoons **olive oil**
2 tablespoons **balsamic**
  vinegar

Put the tomatoes and mushrooms in a roasting tin, drizzle with about 2 tablespoons oil, season with salt and pepper, and cook in a preheated oven, 180°C (350°F), Gas Mark 4, for 10 minutes.

Put the courgettes and asparagus in a large bowl, meanwhile. Drizzle with olive oil and a pinch of salt and pepper. Heat a griddle pan over a high heat, and grill the asparagus and courgettes until starting to colour. Transfer the asparagus and courgettes to the oven with the tomatoes and mushrooms and cook for 6–8 minutes.

Use a sheet of kitchen paper to wipe the griddle pan clean. Pat the cheese slices dry with kitchen paper. Heat 1 teaspoon olive oil in the pan over a medium heat. Grill the haloumi, turning once (use a fish slice or spatula to loosen the cheese first), for about 4 minutes until lightly golden with grill marks on both sides. Make the dressing by whisking together the oil and vinegar. Stack the grilled vegetables and mushrooms on 4 warmed plates, dividing the ingredients evenly. Top with slices of cheese, spoon over the dressing and serve immediately.

For watermelon & haloumi cheese, cut 250 g (8 oz) haloumi cheese into thin slices. Heat 1 tablespoon olive oil in a large nonstick frying pan over a medium heat and cook the cheese for about 4 minutes until golden and crispy on both sides. Drain and pat dry with kitchen paper. Halve, peel and deseed ½ small watermelon and cut the flesh into small triangles. Toss the melon with a small bunch of chopped mint and the diced flesh of 1 ripe halved, stoned and peeled avocado. Serve with the grilled haloumi. **Calories per serving 298**

fruity stuffed peppers

Calories per serving **421**
Preparation time **15 minutes**
Cooking time **1 hour**
Serves **4**

2 **red peppers**, cored,
   deseeded and halved
2 **orange peppers**, cored,
   deseeded and halved
2 tablespoons **olive oil**,
   plus extra for brushing
1 **red onion**, chopped
1 **garlic clove**, crushed
1 small **fresh red chilli**,
   deseeded and finely
   chopped
25 g (1 oz) **pine nuts**
200 g (7 oz) cooked **wild rice**
400 g (13 oz) can **green
   lentils**, rinsed and drained
250 g (8 oz) **cherry tomatoes**,
   quartered
100 g (3½ oz) **ready-to-eat
   dried apricots**, chopped
handful of **sultanas**
grated rind of 1 **lemon**
2 tablespoons chopped **fresh
   herbs**
100 g (3½ oz) **feta cheese**,
   crumbled

Put the peppers in an ovenproof dish, cut-side up, and brush each with a little oil. Place in a preheated oven, 200°C (400°F), Gas Mark 6, for 20 minutes.

Heat the oil in frying pan, add the onion, garlic and chilli and fry for 2 minutes, then add the pine nuts and cook for a further 2 minutes until golden. Stir in all the remaining ingredients.

Remove the peppers from the oven and spoon the stuffing mixture into the peppers. Cover with foil, return to the oven and cook for 25 minutes, then remove the foil and cook for a further 15 minutes. Serve with a crisp salad.

For fruity stuffed aubergines, roughly prick 2 large aubergines all over with a fork. Place on a baking sheet and put in a preheated oven, 200°C, (400°F), Gas Mark 6, for 30 minutes. Remove from the oven and halve lengthways, scoop out most of the flesh and roughly chop. Make the stuffing as above, adding the aubergine flesh to the pan with the onion, garlic and chilli. Spoon the mixture into the aubergine skins and cook as above. Calories per serving **393**

okra & coconut stew

Calories per serving **421**
Serves **4**
Preparation time **15 minutes**
Cooking time **40 minutes**

375 g (12 oz) **okra**
4 tablespoons **vegetable oil**
2 **onions**, chopped
2 **green peppers**, cored,
  deseeded and cut into
  chunks
3 **celery sticks**, thinly sliced
3 **garlic cloves**, crushed
4 teaspoons **Cajun spice
  blend**
½ teaspoon **ground turmeric**
300 ml (½ pint) **vegetable
  stock**
400 ml (14 fl oz) can **coconut
  milk**
200 g (7 oz) **frozen
  sweetcorn**
juice of **1 lime**
4 tablespoons chopped fresh
  coriander
salt and **pepper**

Trim the stalk ends from the okra and cut the pods into 1.5 cm (¾ inch) lengths.

Heat 2 tablespoons of the oil in a large deep-sided frying pan or shallow flameproof casserole and fry the okra for 5 minutes. Lift out with a slotted spoon onto a plate.

Add the remaining oil to the pan and very gently fry the onions, peppers and celery, stirring frequently, for 10 minutes until softened but not browned. Add the garlic, spice blend and turmeric and cook for 1 minute.

Pour in the stock and coconut milk and bring to the boil. Reduce the heat, cover and cook gently for 10 minutes. Return the okra to the pan with the sweetcorn, lime juice and coriander and cook for a further 10 minutes. Season to taste with salt and pepper and serve.

For easy cornbread, to serve as an accompaniment, mix together 150 g (5 oz) cornmeal, 100 g (3½ oz) plain flour, 1 teaspoon salt, 2 teaspoons baking powder, ½ teaspoon ground cumin and ½ teaspoon dried chilli flakes in a bowl. Beat 1 egg with 200 ml (7 fl oz) milk and add to the bowl. Mix gently until just combined (do not overmix). Turn into a greased 600 ml (1 pint) loaf tin. Bake in a preheated oven, 190°C (375°F), Gas Mark 5, for 30 minutes until firm to the touch. Serve warm or transfer to a wire rack to cool.
Calories per serving 272

spinach & butter bean frittata

Calories per serving **432**
  (not including salad)
Serves **2**
Preparation time **10 minutes**
Cooking time **10 minutes**

1 teaspoon **olive oil**
1 **onion**, sliced
400 g (13 oz) can **butter
  beans**, rinsed and drained
200 g (7 oz) **baby spinach
  leaves**
4 **eggs**, beaten
50 g (2 oz) **ricotta cheese**
salt (optional) and **black
  pepper**

Heat the oil in a medium frying pan. Add the onion and fry for 3–4 minutes until softened. Add the butter beans and spinach and heat gently for 2–3 minutes until the spinach has wilted.

Pour over the eggs, then spoon over the ricotta and season with salt (if liked) and pepper. Cook until almost set, then place under a preheated hot grill and cook for 1–2 minutes until golden and set. Serve with a tomato and red onion salad, if liked.

For Stilton & broccoli frittata, heat 1 teaspoon olive oil in a frying pan and fry 1 sliced onion until softened. Add 100 g (3½ oz) small, cooked broccoli florets and fry for 2 more minutes. Add the beaten eggs and scatter through 75 g (3 oz) crumbled Stilton cheese. Cook as above until almost set, then transfer to a hot grill and cook until golden. **Calories per serving 371**

aubergine parcels with pine nuts

Calories per serving **436**
Serves **2**
Preparation time **30 minutes,
  plus chilling**
Cooking time **12–15 minutes**

1 tablespoon **pine nuts**
1 long, large **aubergine**
125 g (4 oz) **mozzarella
  cheese**
1 large or 2 small **plum
  tomatoes**
8 large **basil leaves**, plus
  extra, torn, to garnish
1 tablespoon **olive oil**
salt and **pepper**

Tomato dressing
2 tablespoons **olive oil**
1 teaspoon **balsamic vinegar**
1 teaspoon **sun-dried
  tomato paste**
1 teaspoon **lemon juice**

Make the dressing. Whisk together the oil, vinegar, tomato paste and lemon juice in a small bowl. Set aside.

Dry-fry the pine nuts in a hot pan until golden brown. Remove from the pan and set aside.

Cut the stalk off the aubergine and cut it lengthwise to give 8 slices (disregarding the ends). Put the slices in a pan of boiling salted water and cook for 2 minutes. Drain and dry on kitchen paper. Cut the mozzarella into 4 slices and the tomato into 8 slices (disregarding the outer edges).

Put 2 aubergine slices in an ovenproof dish, forming an X-shape. Put a slice of tomato on top, season with salt and pepper, add a basil leaf, a slice of mozzarella, another basil leaf, then more salt and pepper, and finally another slice of tomato. Fold the edges of the aubergine around the filling to make a parcel. Repeat with the other ingredients to make 4 parcels in total. Cover and chill in the refrigerator for 20 minutes.

Brush the aubergine parcels with oil. Put the dish under a preheated hot grill and cook for about 5 minutes on each side until golden-brown. Serve 2 parcels per person, drizzled with the dressing, and scattered with the pine nuts and torn basil leaves.

For aubergine parcels with garlic bruschetta,
drizzle 4 slices of ciabatta with 1 tablespoon olive oil and rub with garlic. Toast until golden. Make aubergine parcels as above and place one on each slice, top with Parmesan shavings and scatter over 1 tablespoon toasted pine nuts. Omit the dressing. **Calories per serving 481**

sweet potato & coconut soup

Calories per serving **440**
Serves **4**
Preparation time **15 minutes**
Cooking time **30 minutes**

2 tablespoons **olive oil**
1 **onion**, finely chopped
2 **garlic cloves**, crushed
1 teaspoon grated fresh **root
  ginger**
grated rind and juice of 1 **lime**
1 **red chilli**, deseeded and
  chopped
750 g (1 ½ lb) **sweet
  potatoes**, peeled and
  roughly chopped
600 ml (1 pint) **vegetable
  stock**
400 g (13 oz) can **coconut
  milk**
150 g (5 oz) **baby spinach
  leaves**
salt and **pepper**

Heat the oil in a saucepan, add the onion, garlic, ginger,
lime rind and chilli and cook over a low heat, stirring
frequently, for 5 minutes until the onion is softened.
Add the sweet potatoes and cook, stirring frequently,
for 5 minutes.

Stir in the stock, coconut milk, lime juice and salt and
pepper. Bring to the boil, then reduce the heat, cover
and simmer gently for 15 minutes, or until the potatoes
are tender.

Transfer half the soup to a blender or food processor
and process until smooth. Return to the pan, stir in the
spinach and cook until just wilted. Adjust the seasoning
and serve immediately.

For creamy pumpkin, coriander & coconut soup,
replace the sweet potato with an equal quantity of
peeled, deseeded and diced pumpkin. Cook the soup
for 20 minutes, then process in a blender or food
processor until smooth, adding 2 tablespoons chopped
fresh coriander instead of the spinach. Continue the
recipe as above. **Calories per serving 292**

crunchy thai-style salad

Calories per serving **440**
Serves **2**
Preparation time **10 minutes**

2 **carrots**
1 **courgette**
½ small **red cabbage**, finely
  shredded
1 **yellow pepper**, cored,
  deseeded and thinly sliced
4 **spring onions**, finely sliced
2 tablespoons chopped fresh
  coriander
150 g (5 oz) **rice noodles**

Dressing
1 **fresh red chilli**, deseeded
  and chopped
4 tablespoons **fish sauce**
grated rind and juice of **1 lime**
2 tablespoons **caster sugar**

Use a potato peeler to shred the carrots and courgette
into fine slices. Toss together the sliced vegetables with
the cabbage, pepper, spring onions and coriander.

Cook the noodles in boiling water according to the
instructions on the packet, drain and leave to cool.

Make the dressing by whisking together the chilli, fish
sauce, lime rind and juice and sugar in a small bowl.

Mix the noodles with the vegetables. Toss the dressing
through the salad and serve.

For crunchy coleslaw salad, toss together the
sliced carrots, courgette, cabbage, pepper and spring
onions as above. In a separate bowl beat together
1 tablespoon crème fraîche, 1 tablespoon mayonnaise,
1 teaspoon mustard and a good squeeze of lemon juice.
Stir this dressing into the vegetables, scatter over 25 g
(1 oz) chopped fresh coriander and serve. **Calories per
serving 341**

216

rocket & goats' cheese omelette

Calories per serving **461**
Serves **4**
Preparation time **5 minutes**
Cooking time **12 minutes**

12 **eggs**
4 tablespoons **milk**
4 tablespoons chopped mixed
  herbs, such as **chervil,
  chives, marjoram, parsley**
  and **tarragon**
50 g (2 oz) **butter**
125 g (4 oz) **soft goats'
  cheese**, diced
small handful of **baby rocket
  leaves**
salt and **pepper**

Beat the eggs, milk, herbs and salt and pepper together in a large bowl. Melt a quarter of the butter in an omelette pan. As soon as it stops foaming, swirl in a quarter of the egg mixture and cook over a medium heat, forking over the omelette so that it cooks evenly.

As soon as it is set on the underside but still a little runny in the centre, scatter a quarter of the cheese and a quarter of the rocket leaves over one half of the omelette. Carefully slide the omelette onto a warmed serving plate, folding it in half as you go. For the best results, serve immediately, then repeat to make 3 more omelettes and serve each individually. Alternatively, keep warm in a moderate oven and serve all at the same time.

For cheese & tomato omelette, follow the recipe above to the end of the first stage. Then top each omelette with 15 g (½ oz) grated Cheddar cheese and 25 g (1 oz) halved cherry tomatoes. Carefully tip the omelette out onto a warmed plate, folding in half as you go. Repeat to make 3 more omelettes. **Calories per serving 427**

mixed bean salsa with tortilla chips

Calories per serving **469**
Serves **4**
Preparation time **10 minutes,
  plus standing**

2 x 400 g (13 oz) cans **mixed
  beans,** rinsed and drained
3 **tomatoes,** chopped
1 **red pepper,** cored,
  deseeded and finely diced
6 **spring onions,** sliced
1 teaspoon finely chopped
  fresh red chilli
2 tablespoons **olive oil**
1 tablespoon **white wine
  vinegar**
chopped **coriander,** to garnish
salt and **pepper**

To serve
150 g (5 oz) **tortilla chips**
125 g (4 oz) **soured cream**

Put the beans, tomatoes, red pepper and spring onions
in a food processor and blend until fairly smooth.

In a small bowl, whisk together the chilli, oil and vinegar,
pour over the bean mixture and toss to coat. Season to
taste with salt and pepper and garnish with coriander.
Cover and leave to stand at room temperature for about
30 minutes to allow the flavours to mingle.

Serve the salsa with tortilla chips and soured cream.

For mixed bean pilau, which will work as a substantial
starter or side dish, add 300 g (10 oz) basmati rice
to a pan, cover with 600 ml (1 pint) water and bring
to the boil. Reduce the heat, cover and simmer for
12 minutes without removing the lid. Remove from
the heat, toss in the mixed bean salsa (see first stage
above) and stir in 3 tablespoons chopped coriander
leaves. Replace the lid and return to a very low heat for
5 minutes. Serve hot. **Calories per serving 483**

roast vegetables & parsley pesto

Calories per serving **474**
Serves **4**
Preparation time **15 minutes**
Cooking time **50 minutes–**
1 hour

4 small **potatoes**, scrubbed
1 **red onion**
2 **carrots**
2 **parsnips**
8 **garlic cloves**, unpeeled
4 **thyme sprigs**
2 tablespoons **extra-virgin**
   olive oil

Parsley pesto
75 g (3 oz) **blanched**
   almonds
large bunch of **flat-leaf**
   parsley
2 **garlic cloves**, chopped
150 ml (¼ pint) **extra-virgin**
   olive oil
2 tablespoons grated
   Parmesan cheese
salt and **pepper**

Cut the potatoes and onion into wedges and the carrots and parsnips into quarters. Put in a large roasting tin to fit in a single layer. Add the garlic cloves, thyme sprigs, oil and salt and pepper and stir well until evenly coated. Roast in a preheated oven, 220°C (425°F), Gas Mark 7, for 50 minutes–1 hour until browned and tender, stirring halfway through.

Make the pesto. Heat a heavy-based frying pan until hot, add the almonds and dry-fry over a medium heat, stirring, for 3–4 minutes until browned. Transfer to a bowl and leave to cool.

Put the almonds in a mortar or food processor, add the parsley, garlic and salt and pepper and grind with a pestle or process to form a coarse paste. Transfer to a bowl, stir in the oil and Parmesan and adjust the seasoning.

Serve the roast vegetables hot with the pesto.

mango curry

Calories per serving **474**
Serves **4**
Preparation time **10 minutes**
Cooking time **8–10 minutes**

1 tablespoon **vegetable oil**
1 teaspoon **mustard seeds**
1 **onion**, halved and thinly
  sliced
15–20 **curry leaves**, fresh
  or dried
½ teaspoon **dried red
  chilli flakes**
1 teaspoon peeled and grated
  fresh **root ginger**
1 **green chilli**, deseeded
  and sliced
1 teaspoon **ground turmeric**
3 ripe **mangoes**, peeled,
  stoned and thinly sliced
400 ml (14 fl oz) **natural
  yogurt**, lightly beaten
salt
4 **chapatis**, to serve

Heat the oil in a large saucepan until hot, add the mustard seeds, onion, curry leaves and chilli flakes and fry, stirring, for 4–5 minutes or until the onion is lightly browned.

Add the ginger and chilli and stir-fry for 1 minute, then add the turmeric and stir to mix well.

Remove the pan from the heat, add the mangoes and yogurt and stir continuously until well mixed. Season to taste with salt. Return the pan to a low heat and heat through for 1 minute, stirring continuously. (Do not let it boil or the curry will curdle.) Serve immediately with 4 warm chapatis.

For aubergine & pea curry, heat 3 tablespoons sunflower oil in a large frying pan until hot, then add 4 peeled and cubed medium-sized potatoes, 1 aubergine, cut into small chunks, 150 g (5 oz) frozen peas, 2 finely sliced onions, 2 crushed garlic cloves, 1 tablespoon ginger paste and 2 tablespoons medium curry powder. Stir-fry for 3–4 minutes or until the onion has softened and is turning golden, then pour in 600 ml (1 pint) vegetable stock and cook for 10–15 minutes or until the stock has reduced. Stir in 150 ml (¼ pint) crème fraîche and serve with a mini naan bread. **Calories per serving 482**

tomato, avocado & peach salad

Calories per serving **477**
Serves **4**
Preparation time **15 minutes,**
  plus cooling
Cooking time **20 minutes**

4 **plum tomatoes,** sliced
1 **avocado,** peeled, stoned
  and sliced
200 g (7 oz) **buffalo**
  mozzarella cheese, sliced
1 ripe **peach,** stoned and
  diced
50 g (2 oz) pitted **black olives**
1 **fresh red chilli,** deseeded
  and finely chopped
3 tablespoons **extra-virgin**
  olive oil
juice of **1 lime**
1 tablespoon chopped fresh
  coriander
salt and **pepper**

Balsamic glaze
600 ml (1 pint) **balsamic**
  vinegar

First make the balsamic glaze. Pour the vinegar into
a saucepan and bring to the boil. Reduce the heat and
simmer gently for 20 minutes, or until reduced to about
150 ml (¼ pint). Leave to cool completely.

Arrange the tomatoes, avocado and mozzarella on a
large platter. Combine the peach, olives, chilli, oil, lime
juice, coriander and salt and pepper in a bowl, stir well
and spoon over the salad.

Drizzle the salad with the balsamic glaze and serve.

For classic Italian tricolore salad, arrange 4 sliced
plum tomatoes, 1 sliced avocado, 200 g (7 oz) sliced
buffalo mozzarella and a few torn basil leaves on a
platter. Drizzle over some extra-virgin olive oil and a little
white wine vinegar, and season with salt and cracked
black pepper. **Calories per serving 324**

roasted peppers with quinoa

Calories per serving **489**
Serves **4**
Preparation time **15 minutes**
Cooking time **45 minutes**

2 **romano** or **long red
  peppers**, halved, cored
  and deseeded
2 large **yellow peppers**,
  halved, cored and deseeded
20 **red** and **yellow cherry
  tomatoes**, halved
1 teaspoon **cumin seeds**
2 tablespoons **olive oil**
200 g (7 oz) **quinoa**
1 **onion**, finely chopped
½ teaspoon **ground ginger**
1 teaspoon **paprika**
pinch of **nutmeg**
50 g (2 oz) **ready-to-eat dried
  apricots**, chopped
50 g (2 oz) **stoned dates**,
  chopped
50 g (2 oz) shelled **pistachio
  nuts**
25 g (1 oz) **flaked almonds**,
  toasted, plus extra to garnish
2 **spring onions**, finely sliced
salt and **pepper**

Fill the red peppers with the yellow cherry tomatoes and
the yellow peppers with the red tomatoes. Scatter over
the cumin seeds, drizzle with 1 tablespoon of the oil and
season well with salt and pepper. Place in a preheated
oven, 180°C (350°F), Gas Mark 4, for about 45 minutes
or until tender and slightly blackened around the edges.

Rinse the quinoa several times in cold water. Pour into
a pan with twice its volume of boiling water, cover and
simmer for about 12 minutes. It is cooked when the
seed is coming away from the germ. Remove from the
heat, cover and leave to stand until all the water has
been absorbed.

Heat the remaining oil in a small frying pan over a
medium heat, add the onion and cook for 10 minutes
or until softened. Add the spices, dried fruits and nuts
and cook for a further 3–4 minutes, or until the fruits
have softened, stirring frequently. Gently fold into the
cooked quinoa.

Heap the quinoa on to 4 plates and top each with
1 red and 1 yellow pepper half. Sprinkle with the spring
onions and extra flaked almonds and serve.

For quinoa-stuffed peppers, make the fruit and nut
quinoa as above. Cut 10 cherry tomatoes into quarters
and mix with the quinoa. Spoon into the halved peppers
and top with 75 g (3 oz) sliced reduced-fat feta or
goats' cheese. Drizzle with a little olive oil and season
with salt and pepper. Place in the oven for 45 minutes
or until the peppers are tender. Serve as above with
salad leaves. **Calories per serving 495**

haloumi with pomegranate salsa

Calories per serving **490**
Serves **4**
Preparation time **10 minutes**
Cooking time **5 minutes**

450 g (14½ oz) **haloumi**
   cheese, sliced
1 tablespoon **clear honey**

Pomegranate salsa
½ **pomegranate**
4 tablespoons **extra-virgin**
   olive oil
2 tablespoons chopped
   parsley
1 tablespoon **lemon juice**
1 small **fresh red chilli**,
   deseeded and finely
   chopped
1 small **garlic clove**, crushed
1 teaspoon **pomegranate**
   syrup (optional)
salt and **pepper**

First make the pomegranate salsa. Carefully scoop the pomegranate seeds into a bowl, discarding all the white membrane. Stir in the remaining ingredients and season with salt and pepper.

Heat a large nonstick frying pan for 2–3 minutes until hot. Add the haloumi slices, in batches, and cook over a high heat for about 60 seconds on each side until browned and softened.

Warm the honey in a small saucepan until runny.

Transfer the pan-fried haloumi to serving plates and spoon over the salsa. Drizzle the honey over the haloumi and salsa and serve immediately.

For avocado salsa, peel, stone and finely dice 1 small ripe avocado and combine with 4 finely chopped spring onions, 1 tablespoon lemon juice, 1 tablespoon chopped fresh coriander and salt and pepper to taste. **Calories per serving 435**

spinach & gorgonzola salad

Calories per serving **495**

Serves **4**

Preparation time **5 minutes, plus cooling**

Cooking time **3 minutes**

1 tablespoon **clear honey**

125 g (4 oz) **walnut halves**

250 g (8 oz) **green beans**, trimmed

200 g (7 oz) **baby spinach leaves**

150 g (5 oz) **Gorgonzola cheese**, crumbled

Dressing

3 tablespoons **walnut oil**

1 tablespoon **extra-virgin olive oil**

1–2 tablespoons **sherry vinegar**

salt and **pepper**

Heat the honey in a small frying pan, add the walnuts and stir-fry over a medium heat for 2–3 minutes until the nuts are glazed. Tip onto a plate and leave to cool.

Meanwhile, cook the green beans in a saucepan of lightly salted boiling water for 3 minutes. Drain, refresh under cold water and shake dry. Put in a large bowl with the spinach leaves.

Whisk all the dressing ingredients together in a small bowl and season with salt and pepper. Pour over the salad and toss well. Arrange the salad in serving bowls, scatter over the Gorgonzola and glazed walnuts and serve immediately.

For watercress, almond & Stilton salad, replace the spinach with an equal weight of watercress. Dress with 50 g (2 oz) toasted flaked almonds instead of the honeyed walnuts, 200 g (7 oz) crumbled Stilton instead of the Gorgonzola, and a drizzle of olive oil. **Calories per serving 318**

creamy courgettes with walnuts

Calories per serving **495**
Serves **4**
Preparation time **10 minutes**
Cooking time **10–15 minutes**

3 tablespoons **olive oil**
1 **onion**, chopped
4 **courgettes**, cut into
   matchsticks
2 **celery sticks**, cut into
   matchsticks
250 g (8 oz) **soft cheese**
   with garlic
75 g (3 oz) **walnut pieces**
salt and **pepper**

Heat the oil in a large frying pan, add the onion and cook for 5 minutes until soft. Add the courgettes and celery and cook for 4–5 minutes until soft and starting to brown.

Add the cheese and cook for 2–3 minutes until melted. Stir in the walnuts, season to taste with salt and pepper and serve immediately.

For curried courgettes, cook the onion as above, then add 2 small, quartered potatoes and cook for 2–3 minutes. Stir in the courgettes, sliced, with ½ teaspoon chilli powder, ½ teaspoon turmeric, 1 teaspoon ground coriander and ½ teaspoon salt. Add 150 ml (¼ pint) water, cover and cook over a low heat for 8–10 minutes until the potatoes are tender. **Calories per serving 198**

index

almonds 232
fennel & almond
soup 114
apples
rocket, apple & balsamic
salad 22
spicy apple & parsnip
soup 108
spicy apple & potato
soup 108
spicy apple relish 80
apricots
smoked tofu & apricot
sausages 80
artichokes
Italian bean & artichoke
salad 182
roasted artichoke &
pepper hummus 192
asparagus 186
charred asparagus salad
with pine nuts 166
aubergines
aubergine & pea
curry 224
aubergine parcels with
garlic bruschetta 212
aubergine parcels with
pine nuts 212
aubergine, tomato & feta
rolls 112
baked aubergines with
tzatziki 164
fruity stuffed aubergines
206
pepper & aubergine
hummus 192
spicy aubergine curry 90
avocado
avocado salsa 230
tomato, avocado & peach
salad 226

balsamic dressing
22, 52

basil 118
beans
baked tortillas with broad
bean hummus 144
braised black cabbage &
borlotti 24
broccoli & black-eye
bean curry 30
butter bean & tomato
soup 184
cannellini with sage &
tomato 34
cheesy squash, pepper &
mixed bean soup 28
fig, bean & toasted
pecan salad 176
home baked beans 128
home baked beans with
jacket potatoes 128
Italian bean & artichoke
salad 182
mixed bean pilau 220
mixed bean salad 176
mixed bean salsa with
tortilla chips 220
quick bean & feta salad
182
Spanish white bean soup
42
spinach & butter bean
frittata 210
squash, kale & mixed
bean soup 28
white bean & sun-dried
tomato salad 102
white bean soup
Provençal 42
beer 136
beetroot
beetroot & chickpea
salad 188
beetroot dressing 58
beetroot, spinach & goats'
cheese salad 82
beetroot, spinach &
orange salad 82
spiced beetroot salad 44
trivandrum beetroot
curry 44

body mass index (BMI) 10
broccoli
broccoli & black-eye
bean curry 30
Italian broccoli & egg
salad 110
Stilton & broccoli
frittata 210

cabbage
braised black cabbage &
borlotti 24
chilli cabbage 50
crunchy chilli slaw 40
crunchy coleslaw salad
216
curried cabbage & carrot
stir-fry 68
curried cabbage & carrot
stir-fry 68
red cabbage slaw 40
speedy coconut, carrot &
cabbage curry 68
calories 8, 10–11
how many calories do we
need? 11
losing weight 12–13
caper & lemon peperonata
54
carbohydrates 17
carrots
carrot & cashew nut
salad 132
carrot & celeriac
coleslaw 132
speedy coconut, carrot &
cabbage curry 68
spiced carrot & lentil
soup 184
spicy squash & carrot
soup 116
squash, carrot & mango
tagine 116
cashew nuts 132
cauliflower
cauliflower & chickpea
curry 30
curried cauliflower with
chickpeas 158

Malaysian spicy
cauliflower 46
spicy cauliflower soup
46
celeriac
carrot & celeriac
coleslaw 132
Cheddar 16
cheese 15–16
aubergine, tomato & feta
rolls 112
baked figs with goats'
cheese 72
beetroot, spinach &
goats' cheese salad 82
cheese & tomato
omelette 218
cheesy roasted peppers
152
cheesy squash, pepper &
mixed bean soup 28
courgette & mozzarella
rolls 112
courgette, feta & mint
salad 36
courgette, pea & cheese
frittata 74
courgette, pepper &
Gruyère frittata 172
figs stuffed with
mozzarella & basil 72
figs stuffed with
mozzarella & basil 72
Gorgonzola, pecan &
pear salad 130
Greek country salad with
haloumi 190
griddled courgettes
with lemon, mint &
Parmesan 126
grilled vegetable &
haloumi salad 204
haloumi with pomegranate
salsa 230
lentil & feta salad 186
quick bean & feta salad
182
rocket & goats' cheese
omelette 218

rocket & Parmesan salad 60
rocket, pear & pecorino salad 22
sage & goats' cheese frittata 86
spinach & goats' cheese frittata 86
spinach & Gorgonzola salad 232
Stilton & broccoli frittata 210
tomato & mozzarella salad 78
walnut & blue cheese salad 168
watercress, almond & Stilton salad 232
watermelon & haloumi salad 204
watermelon, fennel & feta salad 106
chermoula tofu & roasted veg 92
chestnuts
  parsnip, sage & chestnut soup 148
chickpeas
  baked tortillas with hummus 144
  beetroot & chickpea salad 188
  cauliflower & chickpea curry 30
  chickpea & chilli salad 102
  chickpea & herb salad 188
  chickpea & pepper salad 178
  curried cauliflower with chickpeas 158
  spicy lentils & chickpeas 122
chicory
  chicory & baby cos salad 130
  griddled radicchio & chicory salad 168

chilli
  chickpea & chilli salad 102
  chilli cabbage 50
  chilli dressing 32
  chilli kale 50
  crunchy chilli slaw 40
  homemade chilli oil 148
  pak choi with chilli & ginger 64
  pickled cucumber & chilli salad 76
  stir-fried tofu with basil & chilli 118
  sweet chilli vegetable stir-fry 26
  vegetables with sweet chilli sauce 38
chive dressing 60
choi sum, garlicky 104
coconut
  creamy pumpkin, coriander & coconut soup 214
  Malaysian coconut vegetables 98
  speedy coconut, carrot & cabbage curry 68
  sweet potato & coconut soup 214
coriander 214
  coriander dressing 198
cornbread, easy 208
courgettes
  courgette & mozzarella rolls 112
  courgette, feta & mint salad 36
  courgette, pea & cheese frittata 74
  courgette, pepper & Gruyère frittata 172
  creamy courgettes with walnuts 234
  curried courgettes 234
  griddled courgettes with lemon, mint & Parmesan 126

marinated courgette salad 36
cress
  spinach, egg & cress salad 134
croûtons 124, 190
cucumber
  cucumber & dill salad 52
  garden salad 48
  pickled cucumber & chilli salad 76
  strawberry & cucumber salad 52
  tzatziki 164, 178, 196

dairy alternatives 17
dairy products 17
diet, balanced 16–17
  improving 13–14
  vegetarian 14–15
dill
  cucumber & dill salad 52

eggs
  cheese & tomato omelette 218
  courgette, pea & cheese frittata 74
  courgette, pepper & Gruyère frittata 172
  Italian broccoli & egg salad 110
  lentil salad with poached egg & asparagus 186
  poached eggs & spinach 134
  rocket & goats' cheese omelette 218
  sage & goats' cheese frittata 86
  spinach & butter bean frittata 210
  spinach & goats' cheese frittata 86
  spinach & pea frittata 74
  spinach, egg & cress salad 134
  Stilton & broccoli frittata 210

sweetcorn & pepper frittata 172
exercise 11–12

fats 13
fennel
  fennel & almond soup with orange & olive gremolata 114
  fennel & orange casserole 88
  fennel gratin 88
  fennel soup with olive gremolata 114
  fennel, orange & parsley salad 106
  pickled fennel salad 66
  shaved fennel & radish salad 66
  watermelon, fennel & feta salad 106
feta 15–16, 36, 106, 112, 182, 186
figs
  baked figs with goats' cheese 72
  fig, bean & toasted pecan salad 176
  figs stuffed with mozzarella & basil 72
fruit 17
  fruity stuffed aubergines 206
  fruity stuffed peppers 206
  fruity summer smoothie 20
  sweet quinoa porridge with banana & dates 140

garlic
  garlic & caramelized onion bhajis 194
  garlic bruschetta 212
  garlic croûtons 124
  garlicky choi sum 104
  pak choi with water chestnuts & garlic 104

ginger 64
gnocchi with walnut pesto as a starter 160
goats' cheese 15, 72, 82, 86, 218

hazelnuts 166
herbs
chickpea & herb salad 188
herb & yogurt chutney 194

ingredients 15

kale
chilli kale 50
squash, kale & mixed bean soup 28

leeks
cream of leek & pea soup 162
cream of leek, pea & watercress soup 162
creamed leek salad with hazelnuts 166
lemon
caper & lemon peperonata 54
griddled courgettes with lemon, mint & Parmesan 126
lentils
lentil & feta salad 186
lentil moussaka 170
lentil salad with poached egg & asparagus 186
spiced carrot & lentil soup 184
spicy lentils & chickpeas 122
lettuce
chicory & baby cos salad 130
garden salad 48
Thai salad wraps 32

mango
homemade mango chutney 158
mango curry 224
soya milk & mango shake 20
squash, carrot & mango tagine 116
milk 8, 13
fruity summer smoothie 20
minerals 17
mint
courgette, feta & mint salad 36
griddled courgettes with lemon, mint & Parmesan 126
moussaka jacket potatoes 170
mozzarella 16, 72, 78, 112
mushrooms
green curry with straw mushrooms 84
marinated tofu & mushroom salad 56
mushroom pasta salad 174
mushroom soup with garlic croûtons 124
mushroom stroganoff 124
mushrooms à la grecque 174
stuffed mushrooms with tofu 94
tofu & mushroom pasta 94

noodles
one-pot tofu & vegetable noodles 180

oats
porridge with prune compote 140
obesity 10
okra & coconut stew 208

okra, pea & tomato curry 62
olives
fennel & almond soup with orange & olive gremolata 114
fennel soup with olive gremolata 114
pumpkin soup with olive salsa 120
onions
garlic & caramelized onion bhajis 194
orange
beetroot, spinach & orange salad 82
fennel & almond soup with orange & olive gremolata 114
fennel & orange casserole 88
fennel, orange & parsley salad 106
oyster sauce 118

pak choi
pak choi with chilli & ginger 64
pak choi with water chestnuts & garlic 104
veggie stir-fry with pak choi 26
Parmesan 16, 60, 126
Parmesan toasts 100
parsley 106
parsley pesto 222
parsnips
parsnip, sage & chestnut soup 148
spicy apple & parsnip soup 108
pasta
mushroom pasta salad 174
roasted vegetable pasta sauce 146
tofu & mushroom pasta 94
tomato & pasta salad 78

peaches
tomato, avocado & peach salad 226
pears
Gorgonzola, pecan & pear salad 130
rocket, pear & pecorino salad 22
peas
aubergine & pea curry 224
courgette, pea & cheese frittata 74
cream of leek & pea soup 162
cream of leek, pea & watercress soup 162
okra, pea & tomato curry 62
spiced seeded pea & tomato pilaf 62
spinach & pea frittata 74
split pea & pepper patties 196
Thai squash, tofu & pea curry 154
pecan nuts
fig, bean & toasted pecan salad 176
Gorgonzola, pecan & pear salad 130
peppers
caper & lemon peperonata 54
cheesy roasted peppers 152
cheesy squash, pepper & mixed bean soup 28
chickpea & pepper salad 178
courgette, pepper & Gruyère frittata 172
fruity stuffed peppers 206
peperonata 54
pepper & aubergine hummus 192
quinoa-stuffed peppers 228

roasted artichoke & pepper hummus 192
roasted peppers with quinoa 228
roasted stuffed peppers 152
split pea & pepper patties 196
sweetcorn & pepper frittata 172
pine nuts 24, 166, 212
pomegranate salsa 230
potatoes
home baked beans with jacket potatoes 128
moussaka jacket potatoes 170
spicy apple & potato soup 108
protein 16–17
prunes
porridge with prune compote 140
pumpkin
creamy pumpkin, coriander & coconut soup 214
Indian spiced pumpkin wedges 138
pumpkin soup with olive salsa 120
pumpkin with walnut pesto 160

quinoa
quinoa-stuffed peppers 228
roasted peppers with quinoa 228
sweet quinoa porridge with banana & dates 140

radicchio
griddled radicchio & chicory salad 168
radishes
shaved fennel & radish salad 66

ratatouille, quick one-pot 150
rice
mixed bean pilau 220
spiced seeded pea & tomato pilaf 62
tofu & rice salad 56
vegetable & rice soup 136
ricotta 16
rocket
rocket & goats' cheese omelette 218
rocket & Parmesan salad 60
rocket salad with chive dressing 60
rocket, apple & balsamic salad 22
rocket, pear & pecorino salad 22

sage
cannellini with sage & tomato 34
parsnip, sage & chestnut soup 148
sage & goats' cheese frittata 86
soya milk & mango shake 20
spinach
beetroot, spinach & goats' cheese salad 82
beetroot, spinach & orange salad 82
poached eggs & spinach 134
spinach & butter bean frittata 210
spinach & goats' cheese frittata 86
spinach & Gorgonzola salad 232
spinach & pea frittata 74
spinach with pine nuts 24
spinach, egg & cress salad 134

squash
cheesy squash, pepper & mixed bean soup 28
roasted butternut squash soup 120
spicy squash & carrot soup 116
squash, carrot & mango tagine 116
squash, kale & mixed bean soup 28
Thai squash, tofu & pea curry 154
strawberry & cucumber salad 52
sweet potatoes
baked sweet potatoes 202
crispy sweet potato skins 202
Indian-spiced sweet potato wedges 138
sweet potato & coconut soup 214
sweet potatoes & tomato salsa 198
sweet potatoes with coriander dressing 198
sweetcorn & pepper frittata 172

taleggio 16
tofu
chermoula tofu & roasted veg 92
marinated tofu & mushroom salad 56
one-pot tofu & vegetable noodles 180
smoked tofu & apricot sausages 80
stir-fried tofu with basil & chilli 118
stuffed mushrooms with tofu 94
Thai red tofu & vegetable curry 180
Thai squash, tofu & pea curry 154

tofu & mushroom pasta 94
tofu & rice salad 56
tofu & vegetables in oyster sauce 118
tomatoes
aubergine, tomato & feta rolls 112
butter bean & tomato soup 184
cannellini with sage & tomato 34
cheese & tomato omelette 218
garden salad 48
okra, pea & tomato curry 62
spiced seeded pea & tomato pilaf 62
spiced tomato sauce 164
sweet potatoes & tomato salsa 198
tomato & mozzarella salad 78
tomato & pasta salad 78
tomato, avocado & peach salad 226
white bean & sun-dried tomato salad 102
tortillas
baked tortillas with broad bean hummus 144
baked tortillas with hummus 144
tortilla chips 220

vegetables 17
chermoula tofu & roasted veg 92
classic Italian tricolore salad 226
country Thai-style salad 216
Greek country salad with chunky croûtons 190
Greek country salad with haloumi 190

Greek vegetable casserole 156
griddled vegetable platter 126
grilled vegetable & haloumi salad 204
homemade vegetable stock 96
Malaysian coconut vegetables 98
Middle Eastern vegetable casserole 156
one-pot tofu & vegetable noodles 180
pickled vegetable salad 76
quick one-pot ratatouille 150

roast vegetables & parsley pesto 222
roasted summer vegetables 146
roasted vegetable pasta sauce 146
spring minestrone 100
spring vegetable salad 58
summer vegetable soup 96
sweet chilli vegetable stir-fry 26
Thai green vegetable curry 154
Thai red tofu & vegetable curry 180
Thai veg salad 32
tofu & vegetables in oyster sauce 118

vegetable & rice soup 136
vegetable korma 84
vegetables with sweet chilli sauce 38
veggie stir-fry with pak choi 26
winter vegetable & beer broth 136
vegetarian pasta cheese 16
Vegetarian Society 14
vitamins 17

walnuts 234
walnut & blue cheese salad 168
walnut pesto 160
water chestnuts 104

watercress
cream of leek, pea & watercress soup 162
watercress, almond & Stilton salad 232
watermelon & haloumi salad 204
watermelon, fennel & feta salad 106
weight 10, 12–13

yogurt 8, 13
cooling, spiced yogurt 122
herb & yogurt chutney 194
yogurt dressing 40

acknowledgements

Executive editor: Eleanor Maxfield
Senior editor: Leanne Bryan
Designer: Eoghan O'Brien
Nutritionist: Angela Dowden
Assistant production manager: Caroline Alberti

Octopus Publishing Group Frank Adam 95, 213; Stephen Conroy 2, 9, 12, 18, 25, 35, 43, 55, 70, 75, 83, 85, 99, 109, 125, 127, 145, 151, 157, 159, 171, 173, 175, 183, 205, 217, 221, 225, 235; Will Heap 10, 31, 39, 45, 47, 63, 65, 69, 105; Jeremy Hopley 41; William Lingwood 87, 111, 153, 161; Neil Mersh 53, 103, 113; Emma Neish 195; Lis Parsons 4, 6, 11, 15, 21, 23, 37, 49, 57, 59, 61, 67, 77, 79, 81, 91, 93, 101, 131, 142, 165, 169, 179, 187, 189, 197, 200; William Reavell 51, 181, 185; Craig Robertson 199; Gareth Sambidge 97, 211; William Shaw 1, 8, 13, 17, 27, 29, 117, 123, 133, 135, 141, 147, 149, 163, 177, 193, 207, 209, 229, 231; Ian Wallace 14, 33, 73, 89, 107, 115, 119, 121, 129, 137, 139, 155, 167, 191, 203, 215, 219, 223, 227, 233.